# Inquiry-Based Practice in Social Studies Education

Written by the lead authors of the *C3 Framework*, *Inquiry-Based Practice in Social Studies Education: Understanding the Inquiry Design Model* presents a conceptual base for shaping the classroom experience through inquiry-based teaching and learning. Using their Inquiry Design Model (IDM), the authors present a field-tested approach for ambitious social studies teaching. They do so by providing a detailed account of inquiry's scholarly roots, as well as the rationale for viewing questions, tasks, and sources as inquiry's foundational elements. Based on work done with classroom teachers, university faculty, and state education department personnel, this book encourages readers to transform classrooms into places where inquiry thrives as everyday practice.

Both pre-service and in-service teachers are sure to learn strategies for developing the reinforcing elements of IDM, from planning inquiries to communicating conclusions and taking informed action. The curricular and pedagogical examples included make this practical book essential reading for researchers, students of pre-service and in-service methods courses, and professional development programs.

**S.G. Grant** is a Professor of Social Studies Education in the Graduate School of Education at Binghamton University.

**Kathy Swan** is a Professor of Social Studies Education in the College of Education at the University of Kentucky.

**John Lee** is a Professor of Social Studies Education in the College of Education at North Carolina State University.

# Inquiry-Based Practice in Social Studies Education

## Understanding the Inquiry Design Model

S. G. Grant, Kathy Swan and John Lee

Co-published by Routledge and C3 Teachers

Routledge
Taylor & Francis Group

NEW YORK AND LONDON

C3 TEACHERS
College, Career & Civic Life

First published 2017
by Routledge
711 Third Avenue, New York, NY 10017

and by Routledge
2 Park Square, Milton Park, Abingdon, Oxon, OX14 4RN

*Routledge is an imprint of the Taylor & Francis Group, an informa business*

*Library of Congress Cataloging-in-Publication Data*
A catalog record for this book has been requested

ISBN: 978-1-138-04787-7 (hbk)
ISBN: 978-1-138-04788-4 (pbk)
ISBN: 978-1-315-17054-1 (ebk)

Typeset in Palatino
by Apex CoVantage, LLC

# Contents

Introduction. . . . . . . . . . . . . . . . . . . . . . . . . . . . . . . . . . . . . . . . . . . .1

**1  Inquiry and the Inquiry Design Model**. . . . . . . . . . . . . . . . . . . . .11
   Inquiry-Based Practice . . . . . . . . . . . . . . . . . . . . . . . . . . . . . . . . .13
      The Elements of Inquiry . . . . . . . . . . . . . . . . . . . . . . . . . . . . .13
      Expectations of Teachers, Students, and Ideas Within Inquiry . . . .15
   Why Inquiry Matters. . . . . . . . . . . . . . . . . . . . . . . . . . . . . . . . . .18
   Why Isn't Inquiry the Norm? . . . . . . . . . . . . . . . . . . . . . . . . . . .22
   Inquiry in Standards and Curriculum . . . . . . . . . . . . . . . . . . . . .22
   The Inquiry Design Model Blueprint. . . . . . . . . . . . . . . . . . . . . . .24
   The Inquiry Design Model: Bringing Inquiry to the Classroom . . . . . . .26

**2  Questions Matter** . . . . . . . . . . . . . . . . . . . . . . . . . . . . . . . . . . .33
   Inquiry and Questions . . . . . . . . . . . . . . . . . . . . . . . . . . . . . . . .34
   Questions and Content. . . . . . . . . . . . . . . . . . . . . . . . . . . . . . . .35
   Questions and Pedagogy . . . . . . . . . . . . . . . . . . . . . . . . . . . . . .38
      Academic Rigor and Student Relevance. . . . . . . . . . . . . . . . . . . .39
         Academic Rigor Through Compelling Questions. . . . . . . . . . .40
         Compelling Questions and Enduring Issues . . . . . . . . . . . . . .40
         Compelling Questions and Multiple Perspectives . . . . . . . . .40
      Student Relevance Through Compelling Questions . . . . . . . . . . . .41
         Compelling Questions and Caring . . . . . . . . . . . . . . . . . . .43
         Compelling Questions and Honoring Students' Efforts . . . . .44
      Compelling v. Essential Questions. . . . . . . . . . . . . . . . . . . . . . .45
      The Role of Supporting Questions. . . . . . . . . . . . . . . . . . . . . . .47
         Supporting Questions as Content Scaffolds. . . . . . . . . . . . . .47
         Supporting Questions as Intellectual Scaffolds . . . . . . . . . . .48
      Students and Questions. . . . . . . . . . . . . . . . . . . . . . . . . . . . . .49
   Moving Forward With Tasks . . . . . . . . . . . . . . . . . . . . . . . . . . . .51

**3  Tasks Matter, Too!**. . . . . . . . . . . . . . . . . . . . . . . . . . . . . . . . . . .55
   Challenges of Knowing What Students Know . . . . . . . . . . . . . . . . .56
   Purposes of Assessment . . . . . . . . . . . . . . . . . . . . . . . . . . . . . . .57
   The Nature of IDM Tasks . . . . . . . . . . . . . . . . . . . . . . . . . . . . . .58
   The Role of Summative Performance Tasks . . . . . . . . . . . . . . . . . . .60

Summative Argument Task. . . . . . . . . . . . . . . . . . . . . . . . . . . . . . . . .60
Summative Extensions. . . . . . . . . . . . . . . . . . . . . . . . . . . . . . . . . . . .63
Taking Informed Action. . . . . . . . . . . . . . . . . . . . . . . . . . . . . . . . . .65
The Role of Formative Performance Tasks . . . . . . . . . . . . . . . . . . .68
Formative Performance Tasks. . . . . . . . . . . . . . . . . . . . . . . . . . . . .68
Staging the Compelling Question . . . . . . . . . . . . . . . . . . . . . . . . .74
Evaluation of IDM Tasks . . . . . . . . . . . . . . . . . . . . . . . . . . . . . . . . . .75
Moving Forward With Sources . . . . . . . . . . . . . . . . . . . . . . . . . . . . .77

4   Sources *Are* the Matter. . . . . . . . . . . . . . . . . . . . . . . . . . . . . . . . . .81
Sources and Inquiry . . . . . . . . . . . . . . . . . . . . . . . . . . . . . . . . . . . . .82
The Disciplinary Nature of Sources . . . . . . . . . . . . . . . . . . . . . . . .84
Types of Disciplinary Sources. . . . . . . . . . . . . . . . . . . . . . . . . . . . .86
Sources in the Inquiry Design Model. . . . . . . . . . . . . . . . . . . . . . .88
The Relationship Between Sources and Questions . . . . . . . . . . . . .88
The Relationship Between Sources and Tasks . . . . . . . . . . . . . . . .91
Instructional Uses of Sources. . . . . . . . . . . . . . . . . . . . . . . . . . . . .92
Sparking Curiosity With Sources . . . . . . . . . . . . . . . . . . . . . . . . .93
Building Knowledge With Sources . . . . . . . . . . . . . . . . . . . . . . . .95
Constructing Arguments With Sources. . . . . . . . . . . . . . . . . . . . .97
Teachers Supporting Students Working With Sources. . . . . . . . . . .99
Selecting Sources in an Inquiry. . . . . . . . . . . . . . . . . . . . . . . . . . .99
Adapting Sources in an Inquiry . . . . . . . . . . . . . . . . . . . . . . . . . .101
Scaffolding Source Work in an Inquiry . . . . . . . . . . . . . . . . . . . .103
Sources and Literacy. . . . . . . . . . . . . . . . . . . . . . . . . . . . . . . . . . .103

5   Conclusion. . . . . . . . . . . . . . . . . . . . . . . . . . . . . . . . . . . . . . . . . . . .107
Constructing Inquiry. . . . . . . . . . . . . . . . . . . . . . . . . . . . . . . . . . . .108
Questions. . . . . . . . . . . . . . . . . . . . . . . . . . . . . . . . . . . . . . . . . . . .109
Tasks . . . . . . . . . . . . . . . . . . . . . . . . . . . . . . . . . . . . . . . . . . . . . . .110
Sources . . . . . . . . . . . . . . . . . . . . . . . . . . . . . . . . . . . . . . . . . . . . .111
Bringing It All Together . . . . . . . . . . . . . . . . . . . . . . . . . . . . . . . . .111
Looking Ahead . . . . . . . . . . . . . . . . . . . . . . . . . . . . . . . . . . . . . . .113

*References*. . . . . . . . . . . . . . . . . . . . . . . . . . . . . . . . . . . . . . . . . . . . .115
*Index*. . . . . . . . . . . . . . . . . . . . . . . . . . . . . . . . . . . . . . . . . . . . . . . . . .129

# Introduction

Everyday we are inspired by what we see and hear in classrooms: Teachers who challenge their students to ask questions and work with sources to learn about the world around them; teachers who help students actively and enthusiastically engage with ideas; teachers who create classroom environments where students can construct thoughtful responses to challenging questions, and where they can encounter and understand a range of perspectives on the ideas in front of them. Although we realize that such practice is not the norm, we see a future in which schools become places where inquiry thrives. We created the Inquiry Design Model to help bring about that day.

\* \* \* \* \*

Inquiry has long been a popular topic in the field of education. And there has been no shortage of efforts to introduce, develop, and sustain inquiry-based teaching and learning. Talk about inquiry has been plentiful (Bruner, 1960; Dewey, 1902/1969; Schwab, 1978), inquiry-based projects have been proposed (Brown, 1996; Saye and Brush, 2005; Swan, Hofer, and Lacascio, 2008), and cases of inquiry-driven teachers have been written (Gerwin and Visone, 2006; Grant and Gradwell, 2010; Wineburg and Wilson, 1991). Those efforts have generated a certain amount of energy and enthusiasm and have even generated positive academic outcomes. What they have not done is grow roots and flourish widely.

The inquiry-based projects we have seen and the ones reported on in the scholarly literature shine a bright light on the real possibilities for ambitious teaching and learning. This book represents an extension of that past work. More importantly, however, it highlights recent efforts to help inquiry grow deep classroom roots.

Our optimism is grounded in our individual and collective work in and around smart, thoughtful, and engaged teachers and students. It is tempered, however, by the conditions of schooling. Scholars cite several reasons for the rocky ground in which inquiry has been planted. One is that inquiry-based practice is too often confused with *discovery learning*, the now largely discredited idea that students should be given free rein to decide what, how, when, and why they learn things (Alfieri, Brooks, Aldrich, and Tenenbaum, 2011; Kirschner, Sweller, and Clark, 2006; Mayer, 2004). Inquiry-based practice *is* student-centered, but it only works if teachers play a key role in seeding a productive environment. A second reason that inquiry sometimes falters is that few teachers have had much experience with it themselves (McDiarmid and Vinten-Johansen, 2000; Saye and Brush, 2006). Past experience does not determine our actions, but it is an influence to be considered. The case-based research on inquiry is growing, but teachers looking for examples would have found few until recently. One last challenge to inquiry-based practice is the assumption that high-stakes tests demand pedantic instruction. If standardized tests typically measure low-level knowledge, it makes some sense to promote low-level teaching and learning. The research evidence, however, suggests just the opposite: It is the students of more ambitious teachers who score better on large-scale exams (Grant, 2006; Grant and Salinas, 2008; van Hover, 2006). Inquiry *can* become the norm in K–12 classrooms. It will do so, however, only through the thoughtful ministrations of classroom teachers. In their hands, inquiry has a real chance to grow and thrive.

Although it was not the case 20 years ago, the research evidence clearly supports the power of inquiry-based practice. We now have a scholarly literature that examines how teachers employ individual elements of inquiry-based practice such as big idea or central questions, making and supporting arguments, and using a range of sources (Bain, 2005; Caron, 2005; Grant and Gradwell, 2010). We also have a growing case literature that takes readers deeply into the classroom lives of teachers and students as they navigate the benefits and challenges of inquiry (see, for example, Gerwin and Visone, 2006; Grant and Gradwell, 2010; Swan, Hofer, and Swan, 2011). Furthermore, the scholarly record demonstrates that students can do inquiry. Where some teachers might balk at adopting inquiry-based approaches for fear that their students could not succeed, the accumulating evidence shows that elementary-aged students can engage as deeply as their middle and high school peers (Fillpot, 2012; VanSledright, 2002b). Moreover, inquiry need not be restricted to only academically gifted students. Researchers such as Susan de la Paz and her colleagues (De La Paz, 2005; De La Paz and Felton, 2010; De La Paz and Graham, 2002) establish that, with teacher assistance, all students can successfully read and write in inquiry-based contexts. And the fact that all students benefit from inquiry-based practices is evident in the studies of large-scale testing. That literature (Beatty, Reese, Persky, and Carr, 1996; Hess, 2009; Smith and Niemi, 2001) demonstrates a clear and positive link between high scores and inquiry-based practices.

And yet all has not been well in social studies. Readers of this book well know the pall that No Child Left Behind created for social studies teachers and that, on first blush, the advent of the Common Core State Standards only seemed to darken that cloud. Social studies, especially at the elementary level, seemed in deep trouble.

Social studies began its national rebound in 2013 with the *College, Career, and Civic Life (C3) Framework for Social Studies State Standards* (National Council for the Social Studies, 2013). Developed outside of the typical standards-building process, the *C3 Framework* arose from the determined efforts of state department of education personnel, the executive directors of major social studies organizations, and classroom teachers. Led by University of Kentucky professor Kathy Swan and National Council for the Social Studies Executive Director Susan Griffin, the *C3 Framework* was intended to highlight the range of content and skills students need in order to understand and interact with the social world around them.

The most obvious difference between the *C3 Framework* and other standards efforts is the Inquiry Arc, a set of interlocking and mutually reinforcing elements that move from developing questions and planning inquiries to communicating conclusions and taking informed action. Content and skills matter in the *C3 Framework*, but they do not matter in isolation. Instead, they are integrated into the Inquiry Arc in such a way that they become part of a curriculum and instructional whole. The Inquiry Arc, then, is composed of four distinct but inter-related dimensions: 1) developing questions and planning inquiries, 2) applying disciplinary concepts and tools, 3) evaluating sources and using evidence, and 4) communicating conclusions and taking informed action.

Based on our experience as the leaders of the *C3 Framework*, then–New York Commissioner of Education John King approached us in the spring of 2014 to develop curriculum units or inquiries geared toward the *C3 Framework* and the recently issued *New York State K–12 Social Studies Framework*. The resultant New York State K–12 Social Studies Resource Toolkit (www.c3teachers.org/new-york-hub/) is a set of 84 curriculum units or inquiries (six each at grades K–11, twelve at grade 12).

We came to the New York State Toolkit project with a curricular model in mind. The Inquiry Design Model (IDM™) grew out of work we did on an earlier Library of Congress grant. The six secondary-level curriculum modules featured an early version of the IDM Blueprint with compelling and supporting questions, formative and summative tasks, and a range of disciplinary sources. Working with nearly 90 classroom teachers, university faculty, and state education department personnel, we refined the blueprint by adding introductory and extension activities and taking informed action exercises.

With the advent of the *C3 Framework*, we developed a national web-presence to create and house resources intended to support inquiry-bound teachers and to offer them an opportunity to chart their journeys. C3Teachers.org (www. c3teachers.org/) is a network of professionals committed to inquiry. Part of the network mission is publication. With the New York State Education Department, C3Teachers co-published the K–12 inquiries developed through the NYS Toolkit project. It has also published a series of C3 Briefs authored by leaders in the field. In addition to publishing resources, C3Teachers provides a platform on which classroom teachers can blog about their experiences as they bring inquiry to their classrooms (Swan, Lee, and Grant, 2014).

Our interest in inquiry-based practice, then, has two sources. First, as researchers, we have studied teachers and students in classrooms where inquiry is practiced. Our contributions to the scholarly literature, together with those of our peers, are building an empirical base for transforming class-room practice. The second source of our interest stems from the standards and curricular work in which we have been recently engaged. Our involvement in construction of the *C3 Framework* in general and the Inquiry Arc in particular demonstrate the potential for curriculum standards to do more than list a predictable set of content objectives. The New York State Toolkit project offered us a unique opportunity to translate the ideas behind the Inquiry Arc into practical, inquiry-based curriculum plans to which teachers can bring their considerable content and pedagogical expertise.

*The Nature of Inquiry-Based Practice in Social Studies Education* represents the conceptual foundation of inquiry-based practice. With C3Teachers.org launched and the New York Toolkit inquiries published, we offer *The Nature of Inquiry-Based Practice in Social Studies Education* as a way to portray the roots of inquiry-based teaching in general and the Inquiry Design Model in particular. Because every inquiry-based effort described in the scholarly literature features three central elements—questions, tasks, and sources—we describe, amplify, and illustrate these constructs individually and in interaction by drawing on examples from the New York State Toolkit inquiries.

In Chapter 1, "Inquiry and the Inquiry Design Model," we set the context for inquiry-based practice by looking at the scholarly roots of inquiry and the rationale for viewing questions, tasks, and sources as the foundational elements. We then describe the different expectations of teachers, students, and ideas in an inquiry-based classroom; why inquiry matters; and why it is not the norm across all classrooms. Shifting to the larger conversations around school curriculum, we offer a brief history of how inquiry came to be featured in the *C3 Framework* and the attendant New York State Toolkit project. The chapter closes with a concise description of the IDM Blueprint, a one-page representation of the questions, tasks, and sources that define a curriculum inquiry, and with a discussion of eight advantages the Inquiry Design Model offers to help teachers and their students embrace inquiry.

Chapter 2, "Questions Matter," tackles the first of the key elements of inquiry-based practice as represented in the Inquiry Design Model. After establishing the relationship between questions and inquiry, we turn to the relationship between questions and pedagogy. Here, we highlight two criteria that define a "compelling" question—academic rigor and student relevance. Academic rigor refers to the idea that a question is academically meaty and can be approached through multiple perspectives; student relevance demands that questions are related to topics and issues about which students care and honor students' best intellectual efforts. Compelling questions that reflect the twin requirements of academic rigor and student relevance share common ground with Wiggins and Tighe's construct of essential questions. There are differences, however, and we think those differences are worth describing. The remainder of the questions chapter speaks to the important role that supporting questions play in scaffolding the inquiry and the role that students' questions can play.

The second element of the Inquiry Design Model focuses on tasks or the work that students do to demonstrate their emergent understandings and their final conclusions. Chapter 3, "Tasks Matter, Too!," highlights the activities in which students engage as they address an inquiry's compelling and supporting questions. Although tasks can be formative or summative, formal or informal, divergent or convergent, they are always purposeful in that they connect directly to the questions that frame them. We begin the chapter by outlining the challenges that constructing tasks pose and then outlining the various IDM summative and formative performance tasks featured in the blueprint, providing a rationale for their structure and relationships. The chapter concludes with a discussion of the issues inherent in evaluating student work.

Chapter 4, "Sources *Are* the Matter," underlines the key role that sources play in building an inquiry. Sources have received considerable attention in the scholarly literature as the impulse to move away from textbooks strengthens. Using sources, however, is no simple matter, and unless they are thoughtfully employed, they can be as frustrating to students as textbooks.

In this chapter, we examine the general manner in which sources function within an inquiry and the particular ways that they function in the Inquiry Design Model. We conclude the chapter with a look at the instructional uses of sources and the ways teachers prepare sources for use in an inquiry.

In our "Conclusion," we reiterate the importance of each of the individual elements—questions, tasks, and sources—and how these elements work to reinforce and support one another. The chapter ends with a brief description of C3Teachers.org and the benefits it offers to teachers. In subsequent books, we intend to describe and illustrate the design principles behind the IDM approach, and to detail and analyze the benefits and challenges of inquiry-based practice.

## Acknowledgments

The journey from the *C3 Framework* through the New York Toolkit project to this book has been amazing. To craft a set of standards with inquiry at the center and to see inquiry frame a set of curriculum inquiries sometimes seem hard to believe. Norms and expectations, traditions and past practice conspire to support the status quo in schools. Few are satisfied with the overall results, and reforms of every stripe have been offered. Yet the stuff of schooling seems hardened to real change. We suspect the reason for this ennui is that only rarely do reforms get to the heart of education—the interaction among teachers, students, and ideas. The Inquiry Design Model does so.

In constructing IDM, we owe much to the ideas and experiences of generations of educators who were not content with traditional approaches to teaching and learning. Some of those educators are no longer with us, but they influenced us mightily through their collected works. Others, our college and university peers, also contributed through their books and articles and presentations . . . and through our conversations over coffee and wine. Still others, the countless teachers and students with whom we have worked, aided and abetted our projects in ways too many to be counted. This project has truly been a social effort.

In addition to these many colleagues-in-inquiry, S.G. would like to begin by thanking Kathy Swan and John Lee. Real, deep, and sustained collaboration is as infrequent as it is extraordinary; to have two such collaborators is the rarest of gifts. Our work proceeds much as democracy does—with fits and starts; with sudden insights and dubious turns; and, on good days, with humor, patience (mostly), and grace. It has been a treat to work with them. It is also a treat to acknowledge the many mercies my family has extended to me over this journey. Anne, Alexander, and Claire sustain, encourage, and jab in equal measures and with deft touches. I am always and forever in their debt.

Kathy would also like to thank S.G. Grant and John Lee, who have brought purpose and productivity to her nomadic academic life. The *C3 Framework*, the Inquiry Design Model, and the thousand projects in between would not have been possible without their intellect, persistence, and generosity. As S.G. notes, our collaboration is as frustrating as it is gratifying—but it is in the most frustrating of spaces we have learned to laugh at ourselves and at the challenge of teaching social studies well. I would also like to thank the G-men, Gerry and Grayson, who allow me to bat around inquiry ideas at night when they would prefer that I focus on what's for dinner and who is taking whom to drumming or basketball. I am thankful for the many ways they encourage my C3 life.

John, too, would like to thanks his friends and colleagues, S.G. Grant and Kathy Swan, for their creative and persistent work on this book. Some say three's a crowd. For us, three is the magic number. Questions, Tasks, and Sources, it's not just a coincidence. Our journey together has been exhilarating. We trust one another, intellectually and professionally, and those convictions provide me great comfort. None of this would be possible without our families, so I also would like to thank my wife and children for listening to me carry on about inquiry and social studies. Sometimes our best thinking and ideas are born in those little conversations with the people we care about most. Thanks Amy, Harrison, and Maddie for sparking my curiosity.

# INQUIRY DESIGN MODEL

# Inquiry and the Inquiry Design Model

A teacher piloting a second-grade curriculum inquiry on the value of rules told us a story demonstrating the power of inquiry-based practice. She said, "My students and I had been working through the rules inquiry for an hour or so when one of them came up to me and said, 'Ms. Valentine, this has been the best recess ever!'" Holly Valentine is an experienced teacher, but second graders can surprise anyone. Ms. Valentine responded, "That's great, except we haven't had recess yet today." Looking a little confused, the boy asked, "Well, what have we been doing?" When Ms. Valentine informed him that they had been doing social studies, the student shouted, "Hooray for social studies!"

Social studies has not gotten a lot of "hoorays" over the years. Typically judged to be one of students' least favored school subjects, social studies teachers are more likely to hear, "This is boring." Inquiry-based practice may not be the entire answer to replacing "boring" with "hooray," but this second grader's reaction gives us great hope.

* * * * *

Entering their fourth decade, the winds of school reform in the United States continue to swirl. Since the *Nation at Risk* (National Commission, 1983) report, reformers have touched most every aspect of the school experience. Longer school days, new curriculum standards, school uniforms, more testing . . . and less testing—advocates of these and other ideas garner some attention, attract some adherents, and generate some data that suggest an impact. None of these efforts, however, has demonstrated deep, ambitious, and sustained change (Ravitch, 2011; Tyack and Cuban, 1995). Widespread agreement surrounds the desire to make classrooms vibrant places, yet tinkering around the edges has proven disappointing.

Reformers' efforts have been particularly unsuccessful in reaching deeply into the classroom lives of teachers and students. White boards may replace dusty blackboards, moveable chairs and tables may offer more flexibility than their bolted-to-the floor predecessors, laptops and tablets may replace backpack-breaking textbooks, yet the central educative relationship among teachers, students, and ideas remains largely unchanged (Cohen, 1988; Ravitch, 2011; Tyack and Cuban, 1995). The reformer's dream of students charging out of class, heads filled with the day's ideas rather than lists of whom to text first, is just that.

Against this background, one of the most consistently promoted reforms is inquiry. Advocates have long endorsed the possibilities inherent when teachers and students engage in reading, writing, thinking, and talking about important ideas. Advocacy may be necessary for change to occur; it is not sufficient. Of all the goals pursued by education reformers, perhaps none has proven more elusive than inquiry-based practice.

That this condition exists is not for lack of effort. Talk about inquiry has been plentiful (Bruner, 1960; Dewey, 1902/1969; Schwab, 1978), inquiry-based projects have been proposed (Brown, 1996; Saye and Brush, 2005; Swan et al., 2008), and cases of inquiry-driven teachers have been written (Gerwin and Visone, 2006; Wineburg and Wilson, 1991). All of this activity has kept the notion of inquiry alive, but it has not generated the kind of deep commitment among classroom teachers that is necessary *and* sufficient to overcome the persistence of traditional pedagogical practices (Bain, 2005).

Good reasons exist for teachers' cautious responses to inquiry-based practices: Standardized tests typically promote factual recall rather than considered applications (Grant, 2010; Grant and Salinas, 2008; McNeil, 2000); inquiry demands more planning and preparation time (Saye and Brush, 2006); teachers' experiences as learners rarely included inquiry-based opportunities (Hammond, 2010; Pellegrino and Kilday, 2013). This last point may be the most salient: Teachers' apprenticeship of observation (Lortie, 1975) ill-disposes them toward more ambitious practices.

Yet the research evidence is quite clear: When students experience inquiry-based instruction, they flourish (Gradwell, 2006; Parker et al., 2013). As Dewey (1902/1969) predicted, given the chance to interact with real ideas, students thrive. And, it turns out, that *all* students thrive. Another reason for teachers' reluctance to embrace inquiry-based approaches has been the inclination to see them as the sole province of the academically talented. The masses of students, so the inclination goes, do not have the intellectual or academic capacity to discuss issues in depth or to make and support arguments.

The case study literature undercuts that inclination (e.g., Gradwell, 2006); the quantitative literature is sealing the deal (e.g., De La Paz, 2005). Teachers may still resist ratcheting up their instruction, but they will find little in the research base to support them.

In this chapter, we set the stage for inquiry-based practice in general and the Inquiry Design Model (IDM) in particular. We begin by outlining the theoretical origins of inquiry-based practice and describing the expectations of teachers, students, and ideas in an inquiry-oriented classroom. We then highlight the relevant research findings that examine why inquiry-based practices matter and why they occur so rarely. We conclude the chapter with a rationale for why and how the IDM approach addresses the traditional concerns about inquiry and offers a practical approach to building an inquiry-driven teaching practice.

## Inquiry-Based Practice

Although classified as a noun, "inquiry" is perhaps better thought of as a verb. John Dewey's (1902/1969) famous description of the difference between a map and a journey well illustrates the point: "The map does not take the place of an actual journey" (p. 20). There is much to be gained from the study of maps; there is as much or more to be gained from undertaking a journey.

American classrooms have long been more about fact-based maps than they have about inquiry-driven journeys: Education historians would be hard-pressed to identify a time when inquiry-based opportunities permeated classrooms. And yet inquiry has fueled the minds of educators for a long time (Barrow, 2006; Deboer, 2006). It will surprise few readers to learn that the first curriculum area to seriously explore inquiry-based practice was science and that John Dewey, a science educator, was among the first to promote this idea. In a series of publications, Dewey (1910; 1938) made clear the idea that "problems to be studied must be related to students' experiences and within their intellectual capability; therefore, the students would be active learners in searching for answers" (Barrow, 2006, p. 266). Joseph Schwab (1960) and others picked up on Dewey's notions and began building inquiry into science-based curriculum modules (Banchi and Bell, 2008; Barrow, 2006).

### The Elements of Inquiry

Although the subject matter differences between science and social studies result in some differences in the ways that inquiry unfold, three common elements surface. First, inquiry-based practice begins with a question (Bain, 2005; Bell, Urhahne, Schanze, and Ploetzner, 2010; Grant and Gradwell, 2010; National Research Council, 2000). Whether teacher and/or student generated, questions are a key element in framing a curriculum inquiry (Grant, Swan, and Lee, 2015). And it is the idea of framing an inquiry that matters. Teachers use questions for a wide range of pedagogical purposes; inquiry-driven teachers use questions as the anchor point in making their content, instruction, resource, and assessment decisions (Bain, 2005; Lucey, Shifflet, and Weilbacher, 2004). Those questions go by many names—central, essential, big idea, or compelling. In each case, however, it is the question that defines the thrust of the inquiry rather than a topic, a list of facts, or the first page of the textbook chapter. As Pellegrino and Kilday (2013) note, "learning by seeking information through questioning heightens student interest and allows for creative investigations and deep analysis" (p. 3).

The second element of inquiry-based practice comes at the end of an inquiry—a summative task that involves the making and supporting of arguments (Bell et al., 2010; Swan, Lee, and Grant, 2015). Any formative tasks that teachers create throughout an inquiry can vary considerably, but an inquiry formally ends when students construct an evidence-based argument that addresses the overarching question. Constructing arguments does not obviate the possibility of using traditional assessments such as multiple-choice and short-answer tests. After all, there is no perfect assessment (Grant, 2016). In inquiry-based practice, however, the emphasis is on the key relationship between question and argument—a good question deserves the opportunity to be answered and defended.

Finally, inquiry-based practice demands a third element—sources. If students are to explore the content behind a question and provide support for their arguments, then they need access to a rich and wide array of source material (Lee, Swan, and Grant, 2015; Monte-Sano, De La Paz, and Felton, 2014). Many of those sources will be text-based—diaries, laws, newspapers, histories; others will run the gamut from artwork to tools to movies to maps. There is simply no excuse for teachers today to rely on a single source. Access to a world of sources brings its own pedagogical problems (e.g., corroborating sources), but the opportunities to support rich, ambitious inquiry are worth it.

We draw these criteria from the good work done to date around inquiry. Much of that work is centered around the teaching and learning of history, but other efforts have aimed more generally at the entire social studies curriculum. The Amherst Project (Brown, 1996), Historical Scene Investigations (Swan et al., 2008), Problem-Based Historical Inquiry (Brush and Saye, 2014), and the work of Sam Wineburg and his colleagues at the Stanford History Education Group (http://sheg.stanford.edu) demonstrate that, although there is no one path to inquiry, questions, tasks, and sources define a common basis. Other projects such as Man: A Course of Study, developed by Jerome Bruner and his Harvard colleagues (Dow, 1991), and the Authentic Intellectual Work model

(Newmann, King, and Carmichael, 2007), adapted for social studies by John Saye and his colleagues in the Social Studies Inquiry Research Collaborative (Saye and Associates, 2015), tackle a broader curriculum swath, but give considered attention to questions, tasks, and sources.

One other element—taking informed action—is evident in some inquiry-based projects (Morris, 2008; Terry and Panter, 2010; Wieseman and Cadwell, 2005). Rather than an inquiry concluding in an argument-based activity, students in these projects extend their learning by engaging in what Hammond (2010) calls "civics-infused history education" (p. 59). Informed action in an inquiry emphasizes the "informed" element: Students are taking action on a contemporary issue, but they also have the knowledge of how the issue has come to be.

## Expectations of Teachers, Students, and Ideas Within Inquiry

Inquiry-based practice redefines the traditional expectations of and relationships between and among questions, tasks, and sources. Questions are no longer an element of recitation, tasks are more than busy work, and sources are more than convenient repositories of accumulated knowledge. Inquiry also asks more of teachers, students, and ideas. Traditional perspectives of teachers as knowledge givers, students as knowledge receivers, and ideas as static content to be remembered do not hold in inquiry-based classrooms (Bain, 2005; Grant, 2003; VanSledright, 2002b).

Inquiry-based practice goes by many names—e.g., problem-based learning (Hmelo-Silver, Duncan, and Chinn, 2007), wise practice (Yeager and Davis Jr., 2005), and ambitious teaching (Grant, 2003; Grant and Gradwell, 2010)—and it has been instantiated in a range of programs—Man: A Course of Study (Dow, 1970), the Amherst Project (Brown, 1996), Historical Scene Investigations (Swan et al., 2008), and Problem-Based Historical Inquiry (Saye and Brush, 2005; Saye and Brush, 2006). To be sure, there are differences across these efforts to define inquiry-based practices, but commonalities reign.

One of those commonalties involves a different role for teachers. Playing only the traditional part of knowledge giver undercuts the dynamic quality of the work done in inquiry-based classrooms. Rather than holding access to all the necessary knowledge and doling it out in bite-sized bits, inquiry-based teachers see their role as one of facilitating the work of their students (Grant, 2003; Hmelo-Silver et al., 2007; Saye and Brush, 2006). By creating an environment in which students can engage with ideas, inquiry-based teachers create the classroom space in which responsibility for learning shifts from teacher to student.

Creating such an environment is but one of the characteristics of teachers intent on crafting inquiry-based practices. The shift to knowledge facilitator signals a new level of trust between teachers and students. Too often, in traditional classrooms, teachers see students as a collection of deficits—inadequate knowledge, underdeveloped skills, and weak disposition to work hard. Inquiry is hard work and, as novices, students will blunder—they overlook key information, they forget to provide evidence for their claims, they craft weak arguments (De La Paz, 2005; De La Paz and Felton, 2010; Lesh, 2011; Swartz, 2008; VanSledright, 2002b). Knowing this, their teachers need to trust that their students will persevere and progress because they are engaged in meaningful work (Grant, 2013b). Teachers also need to accept the fact that inquiry-based practice is riskier than traditional approaches (Bain, 2005; van Hover, 2006; van Hover and Heinecke, 2005).

Given a changing teacher role, it is no surprise that student roles also have to change in an inquiry-based classroom. One of the big changes is that students need to trust that their teachers will construct learning opportunities that give them more freedom . . . and more responsibility. Just as traditional teachers grow comfortable giving knowledge, traditional students grow comfortable receiving it (Dewey, 1902/1969). Students work harder in inquiry-based classrooms; they have to trust their teachers that the extra effort will be worth it. The idea of *active* students involves more than physical movement: Students engaged in an inquiry do receive knowledge from teachers and texts, but they also construct knowledge as they put ideas together in ways that represent their emergent understandings (Hammond and Manfra, 2009; Lesh, 2011; Saye and Brush, 2007; Swan et al., 2008).

Ideas also take on a new role in inquiry-based classrooms. The debate over whether students need content or skills is over; they need both (Grant, 2013a, 2013b). The scope of that content and those skills, however, has widened considerably. On the content side, it is no longer acceptable to present a single, streamlined, just-the-facts narrative. Constructing such narratives is efficient, but doing so undercuts the idea that students need more access to ideas rather than less (Grant, 2003; Swan et al., 2008). Those ideas include facts, concepts, and generalizations that cross disciplinary boundaries. Students also need access to more rather than fewer perspectives. Putting students in touch with disciplinary concepts creates opportunities for more perspectives, as geographers may offer a different view on an issue than do economists, historians, or political scientists. Within each field, however, diversity of perspective is also to be expected. Consensus views can emerge within disciplines, but there is no issue on which historians (or their social science peers) converge completely (Novick, 1988). So students need to see that differing perspectives offer alternative means of exploring a topic.

Just as the content and perspectives on content expand in an inquiry-based classroom, so too do the skills that students need. Some of those skills are disciplinary (Doolittle, Hicks, and Ewing, 2004; Monte-Sano et al., 2014).

For example, students need to understand and employ historical thinking skills such as contextualization and corroboration. Other skills are rooted in literacy, as reading and writing with sources is key to inquiry-based practice (Lee and Swan, 2013). And still other skills are technological (Lee, Doolittle, and Hicks, 2008). Access to sources through the Internet has dramatically increased the kinds of material students can use to understand a topic. That access, however, demands that students acquire a range of skills in order to become digitally literate (Hicks, van Hover, Washington, and Lee, 2011; Lee, 2010; Lee, Manfra, and List, 2013; Swan and Hofer, 2013; Swan et al., 2011).

Two other points about how ideas are treated in an inquiry-based classroom are in order. The first concerns the ideas that students bring to an inquiry; the second concerns the nature of ideas.

Constructivist theory demonstrates the importance of understanding how students make sense of ideas in general and the key role that their prior knowledge plays in particular (Bruner, 1990; McKeown and Beck, 1994; Willingham, 2007). The ideas represented in history and the social science disciplines form the content and conceptual basis for an inquiry. Yet students do not appropriate those ideas whole cloth. Instead, students use their prior knowledge to filter, shape, and revise the ideas that they encounter. Not all of their efforts will be successful; sometimes the result is a kind of factual stew (VanSledright, 1995). Still, understanding that students have ideas independent of the sources that teachers put in front of them and that those ideas will intersect in a variety of ways with those sources is key to understanding how any inquiry may develop.

Finally, a level of uncertainty characterizes inquiry-based units. Because they involve real-world questions and contexts that are ill-defined and because they are dependent on students' prior knowledge, inquiry can assume a kind of intellectual messiness (Lesh, 2011; Wieseman and Cadwell, 2005; Willingham, 2007). Inquiry-based practice is not for the faint of heart, but then neither is life. Presumably one of the reasons that students dislike school-based social studies is that it seems so distant from the lives they lead (Epstein, 2009; Schug, Todd, and Beery, 1984). Inquiry may be unsettling, but it is also deeply engaging for all students.

The last point notwithstanding, alert readers will notice that each of these role changes involves a degree of uncertainty. Inquiry-based teachers have to trust that their students will pick up and run with the challenges they set before them. But what if they don't? Students have to trust that their individual and collective efforts will pay off if they invest in more challenging projects. But what if they don't? The uncertainty that teachers and students face finds expression in the notion that ideas are uncertain too. The idea of a fact offers some cognitive comfort; accumulating factual knowledge, however, is but one part of an inquiry-based classroom. The ideas that students read, write, listen to, and talk about are, like life, always unfolding. So, although questions, tasks, and sources define the fundamental elements of classroom-based inquiry, bringing those elements together and to life demands a new set of roles for teachers, students, and ideas.

## Why Inquiry Matters

The long history of advocating for inquiry is matched by the short list of cases of inquiry in practice. We explore the historical headwinds inquiry-based practice has faced in the next section. Here, however, we focus on the small but powerful literature that says inquiry is worth it. Many benefits accrue in inquiry-based classrooms. In the end, however, only one thing matters—students gain the kinds of knowledge and skills and dispositions that fail to flourish in traditional classrooms.

The literature base advocating inquiry is huge; a relatively small part of that literature, however, examines what inquiry can look like within the walls of a classroom. An even smaller number of studies look at the ways that teachers and students navigate through ideas in the form of questions, tasks, and sources. Most studies explore one or more elements; rarely do they encompass the entirety of an inquiry-based classroom.

One case that does is high school teacher Trisha Davis's (2010) account of her transformation to inquiry-based practice. Davis's classroom challenges begin with the composition of her urban classroom, which reflects high numbers of racially and ethnically diverse students, many of whom come from low income families and have extra academic needs. Such a diverse range of students might unnerve some teachers; Davis simply teaches the students who are in front of her. That said, her instructional methods are anything but simple. Davis uses a big idea question to frame her teaching units, she puts lots of sources in front of students, and she assigns a range of tasks. She also gets big results on the state standardized test, as both her general and special education students well out-perform expectations.

Davis's story is not an isolated case. Although it is one of the few where we can see deeply into a teacher's practice *and* know how students perform on classroom-based and large-scale assessments, it stands alongside many cases of teachers who employ inquiry-based practices (Foels, 2010; Gradwell, 2006; Swan et al., 2011). Although there is considerable overlap, those cases can be categorized to highlight the three elements of inquiry—questions, tasks, and sources—noted earlier.

A growing number of research studies describe teachers using *questions* as a means of building inquiry into their instructional practices. Questions are a common element in social studies classrooms, yet most serve instructional purposes only and focus on relatively low-level knowledge and the transmission of that knowledge (Bain, 2005; Lucey et al., 2004). Inquiry-oriented teachers use questions to scaffold their teaching units around a central, big idea, or compelling question (Caron, 2005; Grant, 2013a; Grant and Gradwell, 2010; Onosko and Swenson, 1996). Such questions need not be about bizarre or esoteric topics in order to gain students' attention. In fact, most inquiry-based questions revolve around standard social studies topics—for example, the American Revolution (Wineburg and Wilson, 1991), imperialism (Doyle, 2010), and civil rights (Gerwin and Visone, 2006)—and they are equally as useful in elementary grades (Fillpot, 2012; VanSledright, 2002a; 2002b) as secondary. Even the old standby topic of European exploration can be pursued in more ambitious fashion through the use of a framing question such as "Did an Irish monk land in America about 1000 years before Columbus?" (Ashby, Lee, and Shemilt, 2005).

The most commonly explored *task* in the scholarly literature on inquiry is the evidence-based argument. Teachers use many forms of assessment tasks, but few capture the nature of inquiry as well as the construction and support of an argument (Swan et al., 2015) Arguments have multiple components—a thesis statement, one or more claims and counterclaims, and the evidence to support them. Students can flounder on any or all of these components (Beck and Jeffrey, 2009; Brett and Thomas, 2014; De La Paz and Felton, 2010). The case literature, however, shows that teachers can build their instruction toward argument making. Key to doing so, however, is the use of instructional scaffolds such as the Cognitive Apprenticeship Model (De La Paz and Felton, 2010; Monte-Sano et al., 2014) and Constructive Controversies (Huijgen and Holthuis, 2015). This literature is more recent and is less robust than that which describes teachers using questions or sources. Still, the findings are notable and, when combined with the evidence of students' performance on argument-based tasks (described later), they offer considerable support for the idea that all students can succeed.

One last way that scholars have built a literature around inquiry-based practices involves the use of *sources*. The Internet opened up many new worlds, but one of the best is access to sources of which textbook-bound teachers never dreamed. That access is not an unqualified blessing, however: Teachers must now spend as much time teaching students how to discriminate among sources as they do how to find them (Lee, 2010; Nokes, 2008; Rodriguez, Salinas, and Guberman, 2005; Twyman and Tindal, 2005). Still access to wide-ranging sources and primary sources offers teachers and their students exciting opportunities to inquire deeply into the topics at hand. And the cases of teachers expanding their use of sources are several. Many focus on the particular skills students need to gather, interpret, and use primary sources (Ferretti,

MacArthur, and Okolo, 2001; Nokes, Dole, and Hacker, 2007; Wineburg, 1991), while others highlight the kinds of scaffolds that teachers create in order to help their students gain those skills (see, for example, Britt and Aglinskas, 2002; Tally and Goldenberg, 2005). Using sources other than a textbook presents challenges (Nokes, 2008; Rodriguez et al., 2005; Twyman and Tindal, 2005), and teachers are wise not to assume that sources teach themselves or that more sources are always better (Counsell, 1998; Woyshner, 2010). Still, the research evidence clearly points to the insights students gain when their teachers expand the source possibilities in their inquiries.

Cases of teachers employing inquiry-based practices offer useful insights, for they help us see that inquiry can take many different forms. Maybe even more important, however, is that these cases show us what is possible. A standard rationale for why most teachers eschew inquiry is that they have so rarely seen it in practice either as students or in their pre-service preparation (McDiarmid, 1994; McDiarmid and Vinten-Johansen, 2000). Reading cases is certainly no substitute for experience in an inquiry-based setting, but the cases now populating the social studies literature demonstrate that it is possible in all teaching contexts.

Demonstrating what inquiry-based practice looks like is important: Teachers can hardly be expected to transform their practices based on the advocacy of inquiry alone. Perhaps even more persuasive, however, is the research base that establishes students' capacity for and benefits from teaching inquiry.

Maybe the most telling study demonstrating a connection between more robust teaching practices and students' academic performance is Smith and Niemi's (2001) study of results on the National Assessment of Educational Progress (NAEP) history exams. Put simply, Smith and Niemi show that students who read more than textbooks, write more than end-of-chapter questions, talk more in class rather than less, and have increased access to technology out-perform their more traditionally taught peers. They conclude that, "If faced with a choice of only one 'solution' to raise history scores, it is clear that instructional changes have the most powerful relationship to student performance" (p. 38). Other researchers offer similar conclusions (Beatty et al., 1996; Hess, 2009).

Such findings, however, may not persuade those teachers who sense that sophisticated reading and writing can only be done by older and more academically advantaged students. But if they do look at the research base, they will find much to allay their concerns.

A large empirical literature has developed around students' experiences reading primary sources. As might be expected, such sources challenge even the best students (Lesh, 2011; Tally and Goldenberg, 2005; VanSledright, 2002b; Wineburg et al., 2013). Yet researchers consistently find that, with appropriate teacher intervention, students successfully navigate their way through (van Hover, Hicks, and Sayeski, 2012). More particularly, students demonstrate their capacity to engage in the full range of historical thinking skills when engaged with sources. Researchers show that students can source the authorship of primary documents (Britt and Aglinskas, 2002; Ferretti et al., 2001; Rodriguez et al., 2005), they can contextualize the sources (Britt and Aglinskas, 2002; Huijgen and Holthuis, 2015; Lesh, 2011; Nokes, 2008; Reisman and Wineburg, 2008; Van Boxtel and Van Drie, 2012; Drie and Boxtel, 2008), they can corroborate one source with others (Britt and Aglinskas, 2002; De La Paz, 2005; Ferretti et al., 2001; Monte-Sano and De La Paz, 2012; Nokes, 2008; Tally and Goldenberg, 2005), and they can identify and interpret perspective within sources (Grant and Gradwell, 2005; Hartmann and Hasselhorn, 2008; Huijgen, Van Boxtel, Van de Grift, and Holthuis, 2014; Pahl, 2005; Reisman and Wineburg, 2008; Tally and Goldenberg, 2005). Within this broad expanse of research, however, are studies that specifically point to the capacity of elementary-age students (Ferretti et al., 2001; Fillpot, 2012; VanSledright, 2002b) and academically challenged students (De La Paz and Felton, 2010; Ferretti et al., 2001) to value and to use historical thinking skills when they read.

If teachers are skeptical about the majority of their students' ability to read ambitiously, they tend to be even more so about their students' capacity to produce sophisticated writing. Although the research base on evidence-based writing is relatively small, it mirrors that on reading: With teacher guidance, all students can produce good quality work.

Accustomed to modest writing demands, students' ability to produce evidence-based arguments will develop slowly. Although students bring considerable life experience to the task of making and supporting arguments, the challenge of *writing* their arguments clearly, coherently, and persuasively is evident (De La Paz, 2005; De La Paz and Felton, 2010; Lesh, 2011; Swartz, 2008; VanSledright, 2002b). As with reading demanding texts, teachers need to provide appropriate scaffolds for students to progress in the construction of arguments. If they do, however, the research evidence clearly supports their efforts: Not only will academically talented students grow, but so too will their academically challenged peers (De La Paz, 2005; 2013; De La Paz and Felton, 2010; Ferretti et al., 2001). Moreover, argument making need not be reserved for secondary students; elementary-age students are also able to understand and produce thoughtful, well-supported arguments (Ferretti et al., 2001; VanSledright, 2002b).

Inquiry matters. But it will only matter if teachers embrace both the challenges and the possibilities of transforming their practices. Advocacy for inquiry will not convince them. The growing research base that supports inquiry-based practices, however, is harder to ignore.

## Why Isn't Inquiry the Norm?

It seems a fair question. We have a literature base showing what inquiry-based practice looks like in classrooms and how students—all students—can do the work and revel in it. So what's the problem?

There are several and they are persistent. As noted earlier, the research base supporting inquiry-based practice is relatively new and, in some areas, is relatively small. We find this literature persuasive; so do the teachers we work with who read it. The bulk of practicing teachers, however, are well into their careers and so may not have tapped the burgeoning literature to see how they might rethink their current practices. But even if the research issue were not the case, other factors support the persistence of traditional teaching. First, teachers typically have not experienced inquiry as students nor have they seen it being done by their cooperating teachers or peers. Saye and Brush (2006) argue that teachers' experiences promote conventional epistemological beliefs, traditional pedagogical visions, and conservative dispositions, all of which predispose them toward instructional approaches that are more pedantic than bold. Second, inquiry-based practice presumably takes more preparation time than do more conventional approaches (Hammond, 2010; Pellegrino and Kilday, 2013). Time will never favor teachers, and revising and rebuilding existing units is no small task. Finally, with few exceptions, large-scale assessments favor convergent thinking and, consequently, convergent teaching. Again, there is research evidence that contradicts this conclusion (Grant, 2006; Grant and Salinas, 2008; van Hover, 2006), but it has proven a hard conclusion to break.

Traditional teaching practices persist for a host of reasons, and these reasons are as real and as powerful today as they have been in the past. Few teachers can argue effectively, however, that such practices work well for all students. In fact, the research evidence is most clear on this point: Students unfailingly rate social studies as their least valuable course of study (Epstein, 2009; Schug et al., 1984). Teachers are right to be skeptical of educational reforms, as we work in a field that seems endlessly fascinated with shiny new ideas, whether or not they are well grounded. Practicing teachers may not have read the research findings that point clearly and consistently to the value of inquiry-based practices, but if they look, they will find them.

## Inquiry in Standards and Curriculum

It has been a turbulent ride over the last dozen years. Pushed nearly to irrelevance by No Child Left Behind and the Common Core, social studies educators have seen their field routinely shunted aside. State and national efforts to maintain a footing in the larger school curriculum appear to be working. Troublesome areas persist, yet social studies lives on.

When the story of the *College, Career, and Civic Life (C3) Framework for Social Studies State Standards* (National Council for the Social Studies, 2013) is written, a big part of it will stress the role it played in bringing social studies back into the conversation about school curriculum. The embrace of the *C3 Framework* has been widespread. The National Council for the Social Studies has highlighted it in a series of articles in its premier journal *Social Education*. Hundreds of conference sessions at state and national conferences have explored and elaborated the dimensions of the Inquiry Arc. The website C3Teachers.org promotes the work of some 30 teacher leaders across the United States who blog about their experiences teaching C3-inspired lessons, which has resulted in more than 3000 educators joining the network. Dozens of states and school districts are using the *C3 Framework* to upgrade their state social studies standards and local curricula. The *C3 Framework* has been embraced as the organizing framework for the new *National Standards for the Preparation of Social Studies Teachers* and for curricular projects created by the Smithsonian American History and American Indian museums.

As important as the *C3 Framework* has been in rejuvenating social studies, an even bigger part of the story is the central role that inquiry plays in that document.

The *C3 Framework* is not the first to build inquiry into a set of standards. The Next Generation science standards (NGSS Lead States, 2013) continue the work of Dewey and Schwab in advocating for inquiry-based approaches. Other countries have also been faster at taking up the challenge of incorporating inquiry into their social studies standards (see, for example, Australian Curriculum, Assessment, and Reporting Authority, no date; Hillis, 2008)

Although not unique, the *C3 Framework* stands in considerable contrast to the state-level social studies standards of the last 30 years. The most obvious difference between the *C3 Framework* and other standards is the Inquiry Arc, a set of interlocking and mutually reinforcing elements that move from developing questions and planning inquiries to communicating conclusions and taking informed action. Most curriculum documents in the United States offer a few general standards and then list page after page of content and skills. Some of these standards are better organized and presented than others, but most offer mind-numbing inventories to which no teacher could possibly do instructional justice. Content and skills matter in the *C3 Framework*, but they do not matter in isolation. Instead, they are integrated into the Inquiry Arc such that they become part of a curriculum and instructional whole (Grant, 2013a; Grant et al., 2015). The Inquiry Arc, then, is composed of four distinct but inter-related dimensions: 1) developing questions and planning inquiries, 2) applying disciplinary concepts and tools, 3) evaluating sources and using evidence, and 4) communicating conclusions and taking informed action.

Also, unlike the other U.S. social studies standards efforts, the *C3 Framework* has been built out into a curriculum and instructional model that fully integrates inquiry throughout. That model, the Inquiry Design Model (IDM), takes inquiry as its beginning premise and instantiates each of the four dimensions of the Inquiry Arc (Grant et al., 2015; Lee et al., 2015; Swan et al., 2015). Based on our experience as the lead authors of the *C3 Framework*, we were approached by then-New York Commissioner of Education John King during the spring of 2014 to develop curriculum units or inquiries geared toward the *C3 Framework* and the recently issued New York State K–12 Social Studies Framework (Grant et al., 2015; Lee et al., 2015; Swan, Grant, and Lee, 2015). In the resultant New York State K–12 Social Studies Resource Toolkit (www.c3teachers.org/new york-hub/), we built out the Inquiry Design Model. The product of that effort was a set of 84 inquiries (six each at grades K–11; twelve at grade 12), each of which features the IDM Blueprint. The blueprint structures the inquiries such that they directly reflect the key elements of the Inquiry Arc—compelling and supporting questions, evidence-based arguments, disciplinary sources, and taking informed action exercises (Swan et al., 2015).

## The Inquiry Design Model Blueprint

What does inquiry look like? Though widely touted, the concept of "inquiry" is typically ill-defined and is rarely developed coherently and consistently through school curriculum. Though not the only approach to inquiry, the Inquiry Design Model (IDM) gives legs to this alluring but elusive construct. IDM is a distinctive approach to creating instructional materials that honor teachers' knowledge and expertise, an approach that avoids over-prescription and focuses on the key elements envisioned in the Inquiry Arc.

Unique to the IDM is the *blueprint*—a one-page representation of the questions, tasks, and sources that define a curriculum inquiry. The blueprint offers a visual snapshot of an entire inquiry such that the individual components and the relationship among the components can all be seen at once.

We give sustained attention to questions, tasks, and sources in the coming chapters of this book. Here, we offer an overview of the IDM Blueprint as a way to illustrate the several ideas described earlier and to foreshadow the ideas to come.

In the blueprint in Table 1.1, we illustrate and define the key components (e.g., compelling and supporting questions, formative and summative tasks, and featured sources).

A blueprint provides teachers an economical sketch of the questions, tasks, and sources that students will encounter during an inquiry. As a plan,

**Table 1.1** Inquiry Design Model (IDM)—At a Glance™

## Inquiry Design Model Blueprint™ – At A Glance

| | |
|---|---|
| **Compelling Question** | Compelling questions reflect the interests of students *and* the curriculum and content with which students might have little experience. |
| **Social Studies Standard(s)** | The state standards provide the content and skills foundation for the inquiry. |
| **Staging the Question** | Staging the question activities introduce students to the ideas behind the compelling question in order to generate curiosity in the topic. |

| Supporting Question 1 | Supporting Question 2 | Supporting Question 3 |
|---|---|---|
| Supporting questions are intended to contribute knowledge and insights to the inquiry behind a compelling question. Typically, there are 3-4 supporting questions that help to scaffold the compelling question. | | |
| **Formative Performance Task** | **Formative Performance Task** | **Formative Performance Task** |
| Formative Performance Tasks are exercises designed to help students practice the skills and acquire the content needed to perform well on the summative tasks. These tasks are built around the supporting questions and featured sources and are intended to grow in sophistication across the tasks. | | |
| **Featured Sources** | **Featured Sources** | **Featured Sources** |
| Each Formative Performance Task should have 1-3 disciplinary sources to help students build their understanding of the compelling and supporting questions. Sources can be used toward three distinct, but mutually reinforcing purposes: a) to generate students' curiosity and interest in the topic, b) to build students' content knowledge, and c) to help students construct and support their arguments related to a compelling question. | | |

| | |
|---|---|
| **Summative Performance Tasks** | ARGUMENT  Each inquiry ends with students constructing an argument (e.g., detailed outline, drawing, essay) that addresses the compelling question using specific claims and relevant evidence from sources. |
| | EXTENSION  An extension task present students with additional and alternative ways to engage with the ideas that are central to an inquiry. Summative extensions can take many forms (e.g., a policy-writing activity, a documentary, a perspective-taking exercise) and are intended to stretch students' understanding through more expressive modalities |
| **Taking Informed Action** | Taking Informed Action tasks are designed so that students can civically engage with the content of an inquiry.  These tasks follow a sequence so that students a) *understand* the issues evident from the inquiry in a larger and/or current context, b) *assess* the relevance and impact of the issues, and c) *act* in ways that allow students to demonstrate agency in a real-world context. |

Source: Grant, Lee, and Swan/ C3 Teachers 2016

the IDM Blueprint offers teachers guidance in planning, teaching, and assessing their classroom inquiries. The construct of a blueprint proffers a metaphor for the instructional design process, which is necessarily context-dependent and fluid. As every general contractor knows, blueprints are not the last word; modifications, adaptations, and improvements may well be necessary in order to meet the context and conditions of a specific building site. Similarly, teachers using an IDM inquiry blueprint likely will need to adjust elements in response to their particular students. The pedagogical focus, coherence, and flexibility expressed in an IDM Blueprint support and extend teachers' instructional ambitions.

## The Inquiry Design Model: Bringing Inquiry to the Classroom

Inquiry is not a complete stranger to social studies classrooms. As noted, a raft of academics have written about inquiry, some individual teachers have done inquiry, and the empirical evidence supporting the idea that all students benefit from inquiry-based practice is strong and growing. These efforts demonstrate that inquiry has both a conceptual and a pragmatic place in schools. To date, however, inquiry has been more promise than reality. The Inquiry Design Model offers several advantages designed to make the promise possible.

The eight advantages that we describe here speak to the issues that teachers care about—curriculum, instruction, and assessment, of course, but also teacher agency and expertise, literacy and civic participation, lesson planning and time management. IDM offers no teaching script, it is no set of lesson plans—instead, it is a way of thinking about the many facets of teaching and learning that honors the work of teachers and their students:

1) *Inquiry-based practice rather than discovery learning.* One of the reasons that inquiry gets a bad rap is that people associate it with discovery learning, a philosophy whereby students define, create, and engage in their own learning opportunities. This approach, rooted in Rousseau's notion of the need for a "natural" education, has been carried forward by any number of educational theorists, though most notably by Jerome Bruner (1961). Largely discredited now (Alfieri et al., 2011; Kirschner et al., 2006; Mayer, 2004), discovery learning is an unfocused form of inquiry. As demonstrated, we see inquiry as a *teaching* practice. Inquiry-based practice makes much of the idea that students need to do the work of inquiry, but they do so, especially in the elementary grades, with their teachers' guidance and support.

2) *Inquiry when it makes sense.* Some teachers will want to immediately transform all of their teaching units into inquiry-based efforts, while others will want to play with a few IDM-based inquiries before committing to an extensive revision of their entire curriculum. Given the range of situations in which teachers work and their varying comfort levels with inquiry-based practice, we think that this individualized approach makes sense.

Teachers who want to work through an entire inquiry from compelling question to taking informed action are welcome to do so. We suspect some teachers, however, may want to tinker with their current practices by mixing in one or more IDM elements. For example, some teachers may begin embracing inquiry by reframing their existing units around a compelling question. Still others might supplement their current units on a topic like the Industrial Revolution by adding an opportunity for students to write letters to local leaders about the need to support local industries as a way to experiment with taking informed action.

3) *A focus on key elements of instruction: questions, tasks, and sources.* Teaching is a complex and uncertain activity (Cohen, 1988; Lortie, 1975). The teaching act can be parsed in various ways, but inquiry-based practice inevitably reduces to questions, tasks, and sources. As the rest of this book unfolds, we bring these elements into sharp relief.

4) *The coherence across standards, curriculum, and assessment.* Standards offer direction, but classrooms are complicated places and so standards become more pedagogically valuable when tied to curriculum. Although there are many paths to translating state-level standards into useable curriculum documents, the IDM process in general and the IDM Blueprint in particular offer teachers a coherent bridge between standards, like the *C3 Framework*, and instruction. That bridge becomes especially strong through the implicit and explicit connections between content and skills.

Far too often standards are developed by one group, curriculum by another, and assessments by yet a third. Individually, each of these pieces may be sound, but coherence across them seldom occurs. As a result, such disjointed efforts end up sending mixed messages to teachers, students, and the public. The Inquiry Design Model demonstrates the idea that standards and curriculum can be woven together in ways that are mutually reinforcing. It is an open question as to whether the redesign of large-scale assessments will follow suit, but the new Advanced Placement exams support the messages inherent in the Inquiry Design Model, and early indications of new state-level tests are positive.

5) *A clear connection between social studies and literacy.* After getting over the initial shock of being pushed aside by No Child Left Behind and the Common Core, social studies teachers realize that they and their students have much to gain by appropriating the relevant ideas about reading, writing, speaking, and listening evident in these reforms. Social studies students read a wide range of sources, they write explanations and arguments, they talk about their ideas with classmates, and they listen (hopefully or with encouragement) to the ideas of others. There is a disciplinary aspect to this work, but it is impossible to ignore the clear connective tissue between robust social studies practices and literacy.

6) *Opportunities for civic participation.* Although it has long been advocated as a way to make social studies lessons relevant, opportunities for genuine civic participation have been few. Learning *about* civic engagement is important; doing something with that learning is critical. Key to powerful civic participation, however, is the idea that it is informed. Action for action's sake is pointless; taking informed action in the civic arena means that students have thought through a set of issues, assessed the options for action, and then decided to pursue one or more courses of action in an attempt to address a relevant issue.

7) *The power of teacher expertise and agency.* The idea that inquiry-based practice can be scripted seems silly: Planning is important, but so is flexibility. Instructional flexibility demands teachers who bring content and pedagogical expertise to bear and who are disposed to revise their plans as necessary to best meet emerging student needs.

8) *Inquiry-based practice works.* The research evidence is both clear and robust: All students can learn and learn well through inquiry-based practices. The presumption that only older, academically able students have the chops to do inquiry simply is not supported by the empirical literature. Will younger and academically challenged students need more scaffolding to read, write, and talk about ideas and arguments? Of course. That fact is very different, however, than the idea that they are categorically unable to do so. Bruner (1960) said, "Any subject can be taught effectively in some intellectually honest form to any child at any stage of development" (p. 33). The research evidence bears him out.

Inquiry-based practice is no magic potion, an elixir to be sprinkled on classrooms. It demands much of teachers and students and the ideas around which they engage. When they do, however, powerful teaching and learning can result. Our students deserve no less.

* * * * *

Inquiry is a much-used term in education. Seldom, however, is the idea defined in realistic classroom terms. The Inquiry Design Model does just that by focusing on the three elements common to all inquiry-based practice: questions, tasks, and sources. These elements enable teachers and their students to dig deeply into the range of topics that define the social studies.

In the chapters that follow, questions, tasks, and sources take center stage. We describe each element in terms of the relevant scholarly literature and in terms of how it integrates with the other IDM elements.

# Questions Matter

Social studies is many things. At its heart, however, is the drive to understand how the social world operates; in short, why do people do the things they do? That seemingly simple question and the many others that ripple out from it open a world of opportunity for students and their teachers to explore the many ways that people have lived their lives both past and present.

And there is much to explore and to be curious about, for human behavior may be as noble, single-minded, and innovative as it is craven, guileless, and inane. How and why, when and where such behaviors manifest and the impact that they have define much of the historical record. For students and teachers to approach that record with curiosity and questions is a signature premise of inquiry-driven history education.

The approach taken in the Inquiry Design Model, then, is to frame grade-level curriculum topics around inquiries, and each inquiry beginning with a compelling question. Compelling questions address key issues and topics found in and across the academic disciplines in general and in state and local standards in particular. But compelling questions also reflect the ideas and experiences that students bring to class. Compelling questions represent a rigorous look at the content of social studies; they also represent conditions that are relevant to students' lives. For example, "Who won the Cold War?" could be considered a compelling question because it reflects a genuine intellectual dispute, but it does so in a way likely to spark student interest in that it plays off the idea that winners and losers in wars should be easy to define (Grant, 2013b).

Crafting compelling questions and the supporting questions that help to scaffold the rest of an inquiry can be more challenging than it appears.

Doing so, however, puts students in the middle of legitimate and authentic inquiries, rather than marching them through a series of "just the facts" curriculum units. We have lots of evidence that the latter approach does not work (Goodlad, 1984; Yeager and Davis, 1996).

In this chapter, we key in on the role of questions in the Inquiry Design Model. First, we describe how questions, both compelling and supporting, help frame an inquiry. Second, we talk through the construction of compelling questions and the two criteria they reflect: intellectual rigor and student relevance. We conclude the chapter by connecting questions with the tasks and sources that complete an inquiry.

## Inquiry and Questions

◆ "By doubting we are led to a question, by questioning we arrive at the truth."

*—Peter Abelard*

◆ "It is better to debate a question without settling it than to settle a question without debating it."

*—Joseph Joubert*

◆ "We get wise by asking questions, and even if they are not answered, we get wise, for a well-packed question carries its answer on its back as a snail carries its shell."

*—James Stephens*

◆ "It is not the answer that enlightens but the question."

*—Eugene Ionesco*

◆ "If you do not know how to ask the right question, you discover nothing."

*—W. Edwards Deming*

◆ "One of the very important characteristics of a student is to question. Let the students ask questions."

*—A.P.J. Abdul Kalam*

◆ "The art and science of asking questions is the source of all knowledge."
*—Thomas Berger*[1]

From Socrates on down, questions have mattered. In Plato's *Protagoras*, Socrates claims, "My way toward truth is to ask the right questions." We may never attain

**Figure 2.1** The C3 Inquiry Arc Begins With Compelling Questions

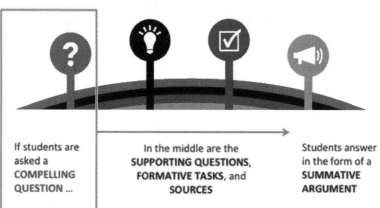

## IDM Follows C3 Inquiry Arc

If students are asked a **COMPELLING QUESTION** ...

In the middle are the **SUPPORTING QUESTIONS, FORMATIVE TASKS**, and **SOURCES**

Students answer in the form of a **SUMMATIVE ARGUMENT**

truth in an absolute sense, but the pursuit of answers to questions defines human curiosity. And in schools, a well-framed question can excite students' imaginations and give real and genuine meaning to their study of any social issue.

Questions feature prominently in the *C3 Framework* and in inquiry-based approaches to teaching social studies. As Figure 2.1 illustrates, questions anchor the Inquiry Arc.

Teachers typically ask many questions during an instructional unit. Most, however, focus on relatively low-level knowledge and aim only as high as the transmission of that knowledge (Bain, 2005). Inquiry-based units begin with questions that promote deeper content understandings and richer student engagement with ideas. Whether they are labeled "central" (Bain, 2005; Brush and Saye, 2014; Caron, 2005; Onosko and Swenson, 1996), "big idea" (Grant and Gradwell, 2010; Grant and VanSledright, 2014), or "essential" (Wiggins and McTighe, 2005), questions help frame an inquiry. Historian Bernard Bailyn makes the case for engaging students in "real questions." Teachers, he argues, should "convey information in terms of questions that are not contrived—real questions that might appeal to students' natural curiosity. . . . If one can go through the major topics in terms of real questions of that kind—interpretative questions—I think you can engage the students" (Lathem, 1994, p. 18). Classroom inquiry can take many forms, but questions need to be part of the mix.

## Questions and Content

The Inquiry Arc from the *C3 Framework* offers teachers an overall approach for their instructional planning. The question of *what* to study is answered by state-level content standards such as the *New York State K–12 Social Studies*

*Framework* (New York State Education Department, 2014), the *Connecticut Elementary and Secondary Social Studies Frameworks* (Connecticut State Department of Education, 2015), and the *Illinois Learning Standards for Social Science* (Illinois State Board of Education, 2016). Identifying the content for which teachers are responsible is important; helping them manage that content, however, is crucial. Questions, both compelling and supporting, offer ways to organize the crazy quilt of content at the heart of social studies.

Content standards can be packaged in lots of ways: They may be expressed through broad, conceptual statements; they may be presented as thematically grouped ideas; or they may be staged as long lists of individual topics. However they are presented, on a good day, teachers may look through them, pausing on an idea or two. On a bad day, they put the standards aside and simply teach their students (Thornton, 1991).

The problem is *not* the content itself. Teachers and their students may prefer some topics over others, and those preferences may not always converge, but the content expressed in state standards typically represents the big ticket items people have examined, debated, and come to consensus on . . . or not. There is no social issue on which all people agree, so the content terrain of social studies is ripe for opportunities to engage students. The problem, then, is how to make sense of the seemingly endless array of ideas, people, actions, and events. Grouping these things under labels like the "Industrial Revolution," "Imperialism," and "Global Communities" helps. Such labels, however, offer teachers and students little in the way of curricular direction—what about the Industrial Revolution, imperialism, or global communities is worth knowing?

Psychologists tell us that we assimilate ideas better when they are grouped, but such groupings need to be conceptually coherent *and* they have to matter. Using questions as a means of framing the content of an inquiry is one way to achieve both of those goals. Historian Bernard Bailyn notes that questions can function as the framework on which to hang the content worth teaching:

> The worst thing, it seems to me, is simply to dish out descriptive history without offering questions, some general ideas, a framework to hang it on. You have to have some kind of hook for the information, or it's just brute force and nobody will, in the end, respond positively to that. (Lathem, 1994, p. 19)

Inquiry-based teaching takes Bailyn at his word and focuses on questions. For example, the Problem-Based Historical Investigation project features questions such as "Was the South justified in seceding from the Union?" (Saye and Brush, 2007). The Historical Scene Investigation materials highlight questions such as "Did Truman decide to drop the bomb, or was the use of the atomic bomb inevitable?" (Swan et al., 2008). And Carl Becker's (1958) high school history textbook, *Modern History: The Rise of a Democratic, Scientific, and Industrialized Civilization*, employed questions such as "Was Napoleon a great man?"

Teachers also use questions in their inquiry-based classrooms. Doyle (2010) used the question, "Does imperialism help or hurt native people?" to construct a unit around that construct. One of the teachers in Wineburg and Wilson's (1991) study posed the question, "What are the sources of authority and freedom?" in a classroom investigation of the factors leading to the American Revolution. "Did colonization of New York result in progress for all?" became the question that Paula Marron used to provoke her fourth-grade students to think more deeply about the origins of their state (Libresco, 2005).

Each question connects to a significant and enduring idea, event, or condition. Although much has been written about resistance to authority, use of the atomic bomb, and the effects of colonization, interest in and debate about these topics persist. A *compelling question*, then, has to be built around content that matters to students, and that is still relevant today. Describing the pioneering Amherst Project, Brown (1996) notes the importance of "structuring units around universal and genuinely open-ended questions" (p. 272).

Let's turn to an example of how a compelling question can frame the content of an inquiry. In the New York State Framework, the Key Ideas and Conceptual Understandings set the broad content parameters for each grade level; the Content Specifications describe the particular ideas, people, actions, and events that illustrate them. Other states take different approaches, but state-level standards and curriculum typically serve to identify a core set of social studies content organized by topic and grade level.

If we follow the New York Framework example through, we see how a broad standard can be transformed into a more manageable curriculum topic in general and a compelling question in particular. Key Idea 7.7 highlights broad-scale reform movements:

Social, political, and economic inequalities sparked various reform movements and resistance efforts. Influenced by the Second Great Awakening, New York played a key role in major reform efforts.

One of the Conceptual Understandings (7.7b) associated with this Key Idea focuses on the abolitionist movement:

> Enslaved African Americans resisted slavery in various ways in the 19th century. The abolitionist movement also worked to raise awareness and generate resistance to the institution of slavery.

And the Content Specifications that follow suggest a range of historical actors, events, and actions that illustrate the content that might be taught around the abolitionist movement:

◆ Students will examine ways in which enslaved Africans organized and resisted their conditions.
◆ Students will explore efforts of William Lloyd Garrison, Frederick Douglass, and Harriet Tubman to abolish slavery.
◆ Students will examine the impact of *Uncle Tom's Cabin* on the public perception of slavery.
◆ Students will investigate New York State and its role in the abolition movement, including the locations of Underground Railroad stations.

Slavery in general and the abolitionist movement in particular represent rich teaching and learning opportunities. Those opportunities become even more powerful when framed by a compelling question. Lots of possibilities come to mind, but we were intrigued by the question, "Can words lead to war?"[2] Doing so allows teachers and students to explore the antebellum period through the eyes of Harriet Beecher Stowe and her powerful novel, *Uncle Tom's Cabin*.

We will have more to say about this question later. For now we turn to the role that questions play in defining the pedagogical elements of an inquiry.

## Questions and Pedagogy

It would be lovely if compelling questions could teach the inquiry by themselves . . . but they can't. Although compelling questions can frame an inquiry, they need an architecture to support and extend them. The Inquiry Design Model features compelling questions and the elements necessary to support students as they investigate questions in a thoughtful and informed fashion. A good compelling question helps structure the content of an inquiry; it also helps establish the instructional components of an inquiry. More specifically, a compelling question helps teachers and students collect, organize, and pursue their ideas through the task of answering the question.

## Academic Rigor and Student Relevance

Compelling questions carry a heavy content and instructional load. But compelling questions do nothing unless they are . . . well, compelling. Sometimes a robust compelling question will come easily; all too often, however, crafting a great question poses a real challenge. The key is hitting the sweet spot between the qualities of being intellectually rigorous and relevant to students.

The idea that compelling questions hit both content and student marks follows a stream of thought from John Dewey to Lee Shulman. Dewey (1902/1969) argued that efforts to focus on content ("the curriculum") or students ("the child") invariably come up short. Teachers need to know the central ideas of their field; they also need to know about the particular students they teach. Yet it is only when teachers see the interaction between these two sets of knowing, when they "psychologize" the curriculum, that good things happen in classrooms:

> Hence, what concerns him, as teacher, is the ways in which that subject may become a part of experience; what there is in the child's present that is usable with reference to it; how such elements are to be used; how his own knowledge of the subject-matter may assist in interpreting the child's needs and doings, and determine the medium in which the child should be placed in order that his growth may be properly directed. He is concerned, not with the subject-matter as such, but with the subject-matter as a related factor in a total and growing experience. (p. 23)

Dewey concludes "thus to see it is to psychologize it" (p. 23), with the "it" being the interaction of child *and* curriculum.

Though his "pedagogical content knowledge" is only slightly less pedantic sounding than Dewey's "psychologizing" the curriculum, Shulman (1987) echoes the pedagogical power of knowing content and knowing students in interaction. Pedagogical content knowledge, Shulman asserts, "represents the blending of content and pedagogy into an understanding of how particular topics, problems, or issues are organized, represented, and adapted to the diverse interests and abilities of learners and presented for instruction" (p. 8).

Compelling questions well represent this lineage of ideas, we think. Although there may be many ways to show a classroom connection between content and students, the idea of framing an inquiry around a question that speaks equally to the "child" and the "curriculum" creates a context in which powerful teaching and learning can occur.

## Academic Rigor Through Compelling Questions

The first criterion for a compelling question is that it has academic value. Although many questions might appeal to students on a superficial level, cutely phrased or outrageous questions will not hold students' interest long. Compelling questions must speak to important ideas and issues, ideas and issues that are worth examining.

An intellectually rigorous question has two characteristics. First, it reflects an enduring issue, concern, or debate in history and the social sciences; second, it demands the use of multiple disciplinary lenses and perspectives. Taken together, these two characteristics support the construction of compelling questions that can be usefully investigated.

### Compelling Questions and Enduring Issues

The content behind a compelling question has to be academically meaty. The Smoot-Hawley tariff (officially the Tariff Act of 1930), the location of coal reserves in the United States, and the story of Betsy Ross's flag may be useful bits of information, but only when they are connected to a broader issue, concern, or debate. For example, although students typically do not have much direct experience with tariffs, they do have experience with the rising and falling prices of imported goods. The Smoot-Hawley tariff *matters* because it is a way to understand how such policies affect our purchasing power. Tariffs in general and the Smoot-Hawley tariff in particular might be the basis for a compelling question such as "Would you pay more to protect American jobs?"

The content listed in state standards typically offer a mix of big ideas and isolated topics. Seldom are they organized around questions, compelling or otherwise. The content terrain of social studies is huge, and so state-level standards writers generally opt for long lists that privilege coverage over consequence. The good news is that those lists can be transformed and rebuilt in ways that support compelling questions.

### Compelling Questions and Multiple Perspectives

Identifying an enduring issue, concern, or debate is the first of two content requirements for crafting a compelling question. The other is the use of multiple perspectives. Multiple perspectives, however, can mean many different things. Here, we offer two versions—one at the disciplinary level and another at the individual or small group level.

As a disciplinary condition, multiple perspectives means looking at an issue through the several disciplines that make up the social sciences and history. Think about it: No social problem comes to us as political, historical, economic, or geographic alone. The thorny issues we face challenge us because they are multifaceted. The dispute over where and how to drill for natural gas seems, on the surface, like an economic issue. Yet there are political, geographic, and social questions that complicate decision making. Students gain insights when they can use history or one of the social science disciplines to analyze a social situation; they gain even more when they can bring multiple disciplinary perspectives to bear.

Building compelling questions around differences in disciplinary viewpoints is one way to introduce multiple perspectives. Quite another is to introduce the possibility of different perspectives from an individual or small group standpoint. Economists, geographers, and politicians may offer useful views on the issue of natural gas drilling. It is important to understand, however, that there may be a wide range of perspectives evident within each of these fields. Individual politicians differ over the value and risk of drilling, as do individual economists and geographers. Consensus may arise in a field (or any social group), but individuals (or small groups) may disagree.

Employing multiple perspectives offers teachers and students opportunities to expand their content understandings. Rather than a facts-only march through a topic, multiple perspectives open the interpretative vault so that teachers and their students can widen and deepen their explorations. A question like "Was the American Revolution revolutionary?" lends itself to an examination through multiple disciplinary lenses: Did the Revolution introduce a major political change while maintaining the status quo economically and socially? Did the Revolution have little economic consequence, but usher in a spate of political and social changes? In short, the American Revolution becomes revolutionary (or not) depending on the disciplinary perspective one takes. But the disciplines offer only one avenue for exploring multiple perspectives. Topics grounded in one or another discipline can also offer rich content possibilities. For example, a history-centered question such as "Does it matter who freed the slaves?" offers the chance to look at how historians (e.g., Ira Berlin and James McPherson) can differ when interpreting events.

Whatever content turn a teacher takes, building multiple perspectives into compelling questions adds a dynamic missing from traditional content units of study. When students look at issues and events from multiple directions, they expand the possibilities for their own interpretations. They also begin to see the content of social studies as expansive, tentative, and alive.

## Student Relevance Through Compelling Questions

Content matters, but it's not the only thing that matters. Brown (1996) highlights the role that the second characteristic of a compelling question—relevance to students' lives—played in the development of the Amherst project:

> We were convinced that the pursuit into the past of questions that students could see reflections of in their own lives—and questions,

> moreover, to which there were no easy answers—would deepen students' understanding of themselves. (p. 272)

The various ideas, events, and conditions underlying compelling questions resonate with historians, geographers, and the like; they also speak to issues about which students care. When students feel caught between rules and consequences, when they see injustice and the rationalizations for it, and when they wonder about the future and their place in it, they open themselves to the promise of a social studies education. Although the ideas and experiences that students bring to class are often naïve, ill-formed, and weakly supported (VanSledright and Brophy, 1992), ambitious teachers can work with those ideas and experiences to fashion powerful questions that connect rigor and relevance (see, for example, Brush and Saye, 2014; Caron, 2005; Grant, 2013a; Grant and Gradwell, 2010; Hillis, 2005; Lesh, 2011).

Teachers ask lots of questions, but not all questions carry the same educative load. Caron (2005) argues that the questions teachers put in front of students need to meet the twin requirements of meaningful content *and* relevance:

> Teachers' use of central questions offers students a more purposeful learning experience because daily instructional activities are directed toward some end-of-unit, performance-based scenario, which challenges students to apply historical information in an informed evaluation of the question. (p. 52)

The notion of a *compelling question* described in Dimension 1 of the *C3 Framework* owes much to this perspective of questions that are "intriguing to students and intellectually honest" (National Council for the Social Studies, 2013, p. 17).

So a compelling question must have a worthwhile academic *and* student angle. Jerome Bruner (1960) argued that "any subject can be taught effectively in some intellectually honest form to any child at any stage of development" (p. 33). Taking this point seriously does not mean that we have to dumb down the curriculum. In fact, it means just the opposite: Teachers *should* teach rich, intellectually robust material. The key is to see within the ideas to be taught those elements about which teachers know their students care. If teachers are able to pull students' interest toward natural resources, the structure of government, or the Boxer Rebellion, they will need to pull from those ideas, connections that are relevant to their students' lives.

The student relevance criteria of a compelling question has two characteristics. First is the need to reflect a quality or condition about which students care; the second is the need to respect and honor students' efforts to engage with the inquiry ideas.

## Compelling Questions and Caring

What do students care about? It's tempting to say that they care only about the latest cell phone, trending fashions, and their friends. The myopia we adults attribute to children and teenagers is too often reinforced for us to give it up. Yet every teacher knows that students can astound them with their insights into human behavior and their capacity to understand and empathize with others. Compelling questions put students in the position where they can investigate the world around them in ways that reflect and resonate with their own experiences.

Teachers tend to have less trouble identifying intellectually rigorous ideas than they do the elements that speak to students' knowledge and experience. It is not that they can't; it's just that they already *know* the content ideas are important, and they take for granted that students will too.

One challenge to creating compelling questions that sing is the tendency for teachers to develop adult versions of what students care about. Students can be encouraged to consider social inequalities, differential power distribution, and opportunity costs. Those ideas gain far more relevance, however, when cast in kid-friendly terms—fairness, bullying, and needs versus wants. Tapping into the construct of fairness, for example, could help teachers construct compelling questions around the treatment of Native Americans by colonial Europeans ("Could Native Americans and colonial Europeans have lived happily ever after?"), property rights ("Can private property always be private?"), and women's social and political rights before the 19th Amendment ("Did the Declaration of Independence include women?"). Other things students care about include *power* (who has it and who doesn't), *relationships* (how do they form and change), *money* (its value and uses), and *consequences* (short- and long-term pros and cons).

Crafting compelling questions that get under a student's skin is key to creating inquiry-based instruction. But there are all kinds of questions that teachers ask: What were the causes of the Industrial Revolution? What natural resources were available to early Native Americans? How do goods and services meet our wants and needs? Such questions may not meet the student relevance criteria for a compelling question—it's hard to imagine a teenager lying awake at night wondering what caused the Industrial Revolution—but they do serve an important purpose in building the content structure for an inquiry. We talk more about such supporting questions below.

## Compelling Questions and Honoring Students' Efforts

Honoring students' best intellectual efforts can be hard . . . especially the day before spring break! But most days, teachers can and should expect their students to rise to their expectations.

And the research evidence is quite clear on this point: When teachers expect more from their students and provide the necessary supports, inevitably students hit the mark (Rosenthal, 1987). We do students no service by undercutting the content or our ambitions. Nobody likes to do busy work, especially if it is not clear what its purpose is. Compelling questions ask students to engage in real and authentic work, and they signal that learning is not easy. But teachers who use them are also signaling that they believe students' work is worth the time and effort.

A question like "Can words lead to war?" asks students to use the historical context of *Uncle Tom's Cabin* and the Civil War as a way to understand the many ways that words—spoken, written, texted—can lead to contemporary problems. Miscommunication is as much a challenge today as it has ever been. Students will recognize the authenticity of the question and will be able to offer multiple examples of times when their best intentions were misunderstood.

The authenticity of a compelling question matters: Students will see through cute or overly clever questions. They may respond at first, but cute or clever questions have neither the substance nor the legitimacy to sustain them. For example, a question like "What's the best Pokémon character?" *might* be a way to introduce the complexities of relationships, but beyond the surface appeal and the inevitable hour-long discussion, the question leads nowhere. Similarly, the question, "Which Kardashian sister is the biggest success?" *might* be a way to discuss family relationships and the value we place on celebrity. And, students will be engaged . . . for a while. But the superficiality of the question is likely to have students shaking their heads and asking silently (or not!) for their teachers to work a little harder.

The point is that compelling question-based inquiries ask more of students than is often the case (Caron, 2005). That they will struggle to meet the raised expectations is a certainty (Britt and Aglinskas, 2002; Reisman and Wineburg, 2008; Van Boxtel and Van Drie, 2012). Honoring and supporting their efforts, however, sends the right messages about the importance and value of engaging in real work (Lesh, 2011; Nokes, 2008).

\* \* \* \* \*

Before we discuss the differences between compelling and essential questions, we would like to make a few final points about the nature and use of compelling questions.

First, readers will recognize that they could use any of the compelling questions at grade levels other than the ones we have identified. We agree: Although the questions and inquiries were written with a particular grade level in mind, they may be employed equally effectively with younger or older students. For example, a question like "Was the American Revolution avoidable?" could be as useful in a 5th or 11th grade classroom as the 7th grade context for which it was developed. The tasks and sources would need some modification, but the question could be compelling to a range of students.

Second, as good as the examples may be, they are hardly the only compelling questions that could be written on those topics. Just as there is no one best teaching method, there is no one best compelling question for an inquiry. Consider these alternatives to the question about whether the American Revolution was avoidable:

◆ Was the American Revolution revolutionary?
◆ What might have happened if the American colonists had lost?

Each of these questions deals with the central topic of the American Revolution, but each pushes in a different direction. The first suggests that students analyze the political, economic, and social dimensions of the Revolution before they make a judgment as to its revolutionary nature. The second question also focuses on the end of the war, but pushes students to explore an optional ending.

Third, thinking about different kinds of compelling questions can help jump-start teachers' thinking. For example, a teacher unsatisfied with her analytic-style question, might consider revising it as one that exhibits word play; a teacher who likes his evaluative-style question but wants to challenge students further might try crafting a problem-based question. In the end, the best compelling questions are those that represent the particular content that teachers want to highlight and the particular students that they teach. That balance can be tricky to achieve, but the idea that a compelling question might be framed in various ways gives teachers a useful set of options.

As ought to be clear by now, we believe in the power of compelling questions to frame inquiry-based teaching and learning. Doing so may seem like a relatively small change, but it is a small change that can pay off huge instructional dividends by giving students a real reason to engage in the topic at hand.

## Compelling vs. Essential Questions

At this point, we expect some readers are questioning the difference between compelling and essential questions. Wiggins and McTighe's (2005) notion of an "essential" question has its roots in the impulse to build inquiry-based instruction. And when we were writing the *C3 Framework*, we strongly considered using the language of essential questions in Dimension 1 of the Inquiry Arc. The more we talked about the idea, however, the more differences we saw between Wiggins and McTighe's construct and the one that was emerging in the Inquiry Arc. We weighed the potential annoyance of creating yet one more term against the opportunity to clearly define the kind of questions we envisioned. The latter view won out and "compelling questions" were born.

The similarities between essential and compelling questions notwithstanding, we see three key distinctions. First, the language of "essential" signals the idea that such questions reflect profoundly deep and foundational human conditions. That's a good and even noble goal; compelling questions *may* reach those ends, but they need not. Compelling questions may push skyward, but they can also be personalized or ironic; they can represent case studies or reflect a playfulness with words. Over the course of a school year, we would expect to see teachers using a variety of compelling question types.

The idea that compelling questions can take different forms leads to a second distinction from their essential question cousins: The latter presumes that they are the right questions for all students in all classrooms. A key tenet of compelling questions, by contrast, is that they are designed with a particular group of students in mind. Compelling questions in the New York Toolkit project and the blueprints that they frame are published as PDFs but, more importantly, they are available as Word documents. We did this with the express purpose of encouraging teachers to modify the questions (and any other blueprint component) to make the inquiries more relevant to their particular students.

A third difference between compelling and essential questions also hinges on the word, "essential." Calling a question essential leaves little room for any alternatives: After all, how can one have more than one *essential* question around a topic like immigration? By contrast, depending on the elements teachers might highlight, we can imagine a range of compelling questions for any topic.

One last distinction, in our view, is perhaps the most important: Although both kinds of questions promote academically rigorous work, compelling questions place equal emphasis on the need to be relevant to students' lives. We have seen essential questions that speak as clearly to content as they do to kids. All too often, however, essential questions seem more essential to adults than to students.

We have long used and advocated the Wiggins and McTighe (2005) approach to ramping up curriculum and instruction so understand that the notes above are not intended to pick a fight. Instead, we offer more in the vein of a friendly amendment: The adjectives we use are less important than the fact that we are talking about questions and the power they can have to drive student inquiry.

## The Role of Supporting Questions

A compelling question serves to initiate an inquiry; a summative performance task, where students address that question, serves to pull the inquiry together. An inquiry's beginning and end points are important, but no more than the elements—supporting questions, formative performance tasks, and sources—that compose the middle of the Inquiry Design Model.

We address tasks and sources later in this book. Here, we describe the key role that supporting questions play in advancing both the content and the instruction in the inquiry. On the academic side, supporting questions scaffold the content ideas central to the compelling question. On the instructional side, supporting questions provide guidance for the construction of the formative performance tasks and the selection of sources and offer a set of guideposts around which teachers can build additional instructional activities based on the knowledge and ability of their students.

### Supporting Questions as Content Scaffolds

Unfortunately, compelling questions do not teach themselves; they need considerable scaffolding in order for an inquiry to take shape. A big part of that scaffolding is the content developed through supporting questions.

Supporting questions are the three or four questions that describe the content relevant to an inquiry. A compelling question indicates the content direction; the supporting questions highlight the particular content and concepts that students need to wrestle with throughout the inquiry.

Let's look at a couple of examples. An elementary-level compelling question "Why can't we ever get everything we need and want?" suggests an inquiry around the key economic concepts of needs and wants. Left on their own, teachers and students could go in a hundred directions with that question. A set of supporting questions helps the inquiry build a coherent path. One set of supporting questions might be:

◆ What do we want? What do we need?
◆ How do goods and services meet our needs and wants?
◆ What happens when there isn't enough for everyone?

The supporting questions in this inquiry move from the concepts of need and want to the relationship between needs and wants and goods and services and then on to the idea of scarcity.

A secondary-level inquiry around the topic of modernization might feature a compelling question such as "Does development mean progress?" Although a set of supporting questions could take any number of tracks, one coherent set might be:

- ◆ What are the impacts of development in Kenya?
- ◆ What are the impacts of development in Botswana?
- ◆ What are the impacts of development in Algeria?
- ◆ Does development impact different African countries in different ways?

Through these supporting questions, we can see how this inquiry develops from the specific examples or cases of modernization efforts in three African countries to the evaluative question of whether development results in actual human progress.

In each of these examples, alternative sets of supporting questions could be posed. Constructing supporting questions is not about generating the one right set. Instead, it is about appreciating the particular strengths and challenges of one's students and working with them to achieve new and more sophisticated understandings.

Two other points surface across the examples: Supporting questions show a content progression, and they build in intellectual complexity. A compelling question puts students in the middle of a challenging and authentic setting; the supporting questions help students assemble the increasingly complex academic knowledge necessary to understand and respond to that situation.

In the needs and wants inquiry, the supporting questions demonstrate a clear progression of content ideas. Students begin with the concepts of needs and wants and then move to the concepts of goods and services. Content-wise, these concepts can be explored independently; where they gain power, however, is when students look at them in interaction and toward a larger purpose. Consider this example: Water, a good, can be defined as a need, but what if it comes in a one-liter Evian bottle with a price tag over $30? Is it still a need or has it become a want? Thinking through these kinds of relationships between and among needs and wants and goods and services enables students to better explore the concept of scarcity evident in the third supporting question. A key economic construct, scarcity makes more sense when understood through the multiple lenses of needs and wants and goods and services.

### Supporting Questions as Intellectual Scaffolds

The supporting questions in the needs and wants inquiry also reflect a progression of intellectual complexity. The first supporting question focuses at the definitional level of two economic concepts. With the second supporting question, students define two new concepts—goods and services—and then they begin looking at the relationship among the four concepts. The third supporting question pulls on the preceding ideas and asks students to apply their emergent understanding in a new context—scarcity. "Scarcity" is not a term familiar to many early elementary-aged students. With the content and cognitive scaffolding of the supporting questions, however, students can see the component elements of needs and wants and goods and services; then they can see how each of these elements plays into the larger issue of managing a situation of scarce resources. The scaffolding of the supporting questions is intentional—students are building their content knowledge at the same time that they are moving up the cognitive scale from definitions to application to analysis.

The supporting questions accompanying the compelling question, "Does development mean progress?," also show content and intellectual progression. On the content side, students build their knowledge base through the use of three case studies of modernization efforts. With that content background, students can then examine the idea of whether or not development is the same in each case.

As they signal the key content of an inquiry, the supporting questions also project increasing academic complexity. The first three supporting questions ask students to analyze the range of outcomes that have occurred in each African nation. As they do so, students begin building comparisons across the cases. The fourth supporting question, then, asks students to synthesize their findings in a way that will help them construct an argument that addresses the compelling question.

In later sections of this book, we describe the interactions among questions, tasks, and sources. Supporting questions and the compelling question that they underscore are best designed in an iterative process, one that continually tests the relationships and coherence among questions, the formative performance tasks, and the sources. Doing so means that each component of a blueprint reinforces and extends the others.

## Students and Questions

The *C3 Framework* makes clear the idea that students should have an active and increasingly central role in the construction of an inquiry's questions. Reaching this goal is not without its challenges. Still, if an inquiry-based approach is important, bringing students into the construction of the defining questions makes sense.

As the authors of the *C3 Framework*, we argue that students can and should play a role in constructing the questions that guide the inquiries in which they engage. In the header for the section on compelling questions are these words: "Individually and with others, students will construct compelling questions. . ." (National Council for the Social Studies, 2013, p. 24). The same kind of heading appears in the section on supporting questions. Attendant to these assertions is the idea that constructing questions is a challenging intellectual pursuit and students, particularly before grade six, will need their teachers' guidance in doing so.

Creating compelling and supporting questions is only one way, however, for students' ideas and questions to play a role in inquiries. Students may not be creating all of their own inquiry questions (as they might for a National History Day competition or in approaches such as the Question Formulation Technique), but their involvement can play out in any number of ways.

▽ One approach is to have students suggest additional and/or alternative supporting questions. For example, in the "Does development mean progress?" inquiry, students might propose a fourth case of an African country undergoing issues related to modernization, or the teacher may drop one of the three cases and substitute in the students' suggestion. Once students become familiar with the relationship between compelling and supporting questions, they may well offer useful alternative or additional questions to further enhance the inquiry.

▽ A second way that students can play a role in question development is by inspiring their teachers to create new compelling and/or supporting questions for inquiries in subsequent years. We have all had the experience where we think we are teaching well only to have a student ask a question that cracks open the topic wide open for everyone. If such a moment occurs early enough, a teacher may shift the focus of the inquiry's compelling question. More likely, however, the teacher will file away this question for next year's class (after complimenting the student first!).

▽ One last opportunity for students to shape an inquiry's questions takes courage: Asking students to critique and modify the compelling question that the teacher created. Writing compelling questions that are really compelling is hard work. Teachers may craft a perfectly sound inquiry but feel that the compelling question is not quite there. In that case, it might be useful simply to ask the students to make it so. Chances are they will. And in doing so, they are likely to learn something about how to construct such questions, understandings that will reap rewards later as they become more adept at developing their own questions.

\* \* \* \* \*

Taken together, compelling and supporting questions highlight the content ideas and issues with which teachers and students can engage. As such, they provide the intellectual architecture for an inquiry. There is no one right compelling question for a topic; nor is there only one way to construct and sequence the supporting questions. "Can words lead to war?" and the attendant supporting questions have been vetted by a range of teachers and academics. That is not to say, however, that others might not develop equally engaging sets of questions. Others may tweak the compelling question, rearrange the sequence of supporting questions, insert additional questions, or even substitute in a whole new series. The IDM approach reflects the fundamental premise that there is no substitute for teachers' knowledge and expertise. Inquiries only come alive in classrooms when teachers and their students make them their own.

## Moving Forward With Tasks

A central premise of the IDM approach is that, if we ask a truly compelling question, then it will be worth students' time and effort to answer it. Supporting questions may be answered through lists, descriptions, and explanations. Compelling questions, however, demand the making and supporting of arguments. A question like "Did the Roman empire fall?" presumes a yes or no response (or a "yes, but" or "no, but"). Each student's answer forms the beginning of her or his argument. That argument only gains shape and importance, however, as the claims and evidence supporting the answer are developed. Making and supporting arguments and drawing on evidence from disciplinary sources, then, form the basis for the next section of this book.

## Note

1  Authors of quotes: Peter Abelard, French philosopher, 1079–1142; Joseph Joubert, French writer, 1754–1824; James Stephens, Irish poet, 1880–1950; Eugene Ionesco, French dramatist, 1909–1994; W. Edwards Deming, American scientist, 1900–1993; A.P.J. Abdul Kalam, Indian scientist, 1931–present; Thomas Berger, American novelist, 1924–2014
2  The inquiry referred to here and those referenced in the rest of this book can be found at http://c3teachers.org/inquiries.

# Tasks Matter, Too!

If questions spark an inquiry, tasks provide the opportunity to make those questions have consequence. Compelling questions, like "Where are we?," "Can words lead to war?," and "Am I going to vote?" frame social studies in intellectually powerful and rigorous ways. But students understand the schooling enterprise and want assurances that their academic efforts will be recognized. Tasks provide opportunities for students to work through their ideas and to receive feedback that their contributions to the inquiry process are worthwhile. In other words, it's one thing to spark a student's curiosity; it's another to hold and focus that interest. IDM tasks provide the instructional and assessment spaces that make inquiry matter to students who are engaging with it.

The approach taken in the Inquiry Design Model is to construct a task as a direct response to either a compelling or supporting question. Tasks can be formative or summative, formal or informal, divergent or convergent, but they are always purposeful in that they directly relate to the questions that frame them. Compelling questions are written to elicit multiple perspectives on enduring ideas in the field of social studies, and as such, students respond to a compelling question with an argument that is substantiated by evidence. Arguments can be made in many modalities, but they are always anchored by the larger inquiry question. Supporting questions help scaffold the content of the compelling question with a coherent progression of ideas that support students in understanding the foundational ideas embedded within the compelling question. Tasks that are framed by supporting questions and animated by sources are smaller in scope and formative in nature since they are helping students build the knowledge and skill proficiency needed for the evidence-based argument and the more expressive tasks that follow.

In this chapter, we explore the value and composition of the IDM formative and summative tasks. We begin by examining the challenges of constructing tasks that help students demonstrate what they know and how educators have used tasks to both assess proficiency and build capacity for inquiry. Then, we dive into the IDM summative and formative performance tasks featured in the blueprint, providing a rationale for their structure and relationships. We conclude the chapter by highlighting some of the issues inherent in evaluating student work and looking ahead to the next chapter on sources.

## Challenges of Knowing What Students Know

One of the biggest challenges teachers face is understanding what students know (Darling-Hammond and Adamson, 2014; Grant, 2007; Grant and Salinas, 2008; Stiggins, 2014; Supovitz, 2009). Teachers have at their disposal a variety of assessment tools, but these have varied intents, and none are perfect.

Assessments are broadly classified as either formative or summative. The distinction between the two is often debated, but this ultimately comes down to how a teacher intends to use the assessment (Bloom, 1968). The same assessment may be used for formative purposes—to diagnose and intervene—or for summative purposes—to make a formal, final judgment about a student's competency in a course of study. For example, teachers could have students practice argumentative writing by working through a Document Based Question (DBQ), or they could use that same DBQ as a final exam. That said, formative assessments are usually designed to uncover where students are at a particular time in an instructional unit and are typically focused around a specific skill or concept (Bloom, Hastings, and Madaus, 1971). Summative assessments are generally designed to glean what students have learned across several instructional units and are broader in scope (Bloom et al., 1971).

Within the formative and summative categories, we have a range of tools as well—from formal tools such as multiple-choice quizzes, short-answer responses, document-based questions, and debates, to informal tools such as call-and-response, small group discussion, think-pair-share, and KWL charts. In any class, teachers employ a mix of both formative and summative assessments using a range of informal and formal tools and techniques to measure what students know at any particular time within a course of study.

However, educators often lack confidence that any one of these tools provides much certainty about what students know, understand, or are able to do (Grant, 2007; Grant and Salinas, 2008; Levstik and Barton, 2015). For example, we know that students' knowledge is often slippery, dependent on whether he had breakfast that morning, if she is intellectually engaged with the task, and if he is facile with the skills (e.g., reading, writing, speaking) necessary to complete the task (Grant, 2007; Swan and Hofer, 2013). And, we know that students' ability to communicate their understandings can shift over time (Rogers and Stevenson, 1988; VanSledright, Kelly, and Meuwissen, 2006).

Beyond these hurdles, educators often question the validity of the assessment task (Darling-Hammond and Adamson, 2014; Grant, 2007; Grant and Salinas, 2008; Stiggins, 2014; Supovitz, 2009). Do multiple-choice questions help us understand whether students can uncover historical perspective? The design of a multiple-choice question and distractors can make a problem intellectually complex or just a matter of eliminating obviously wrong options (VanSledright, 2013). Do the skills required for making a digital documentary eclipse the important content knowledge contained in a particular unit? A student's final product may be technically or artistically complex (e.g., Prezi presentation, public service announcement) but reflect a shallow application of the disciplinary concepts (Swan and Hofer, 2013). How does a teacher tease out the individual contributions of a group project to determine what a student knows about the topic? Collaborative assessments (e.g., debates, group presentation) are fundamental to the social studies, and yet they also present a myriad of evaluation challenges for teachers (Stiggins, 1994; Wiggins, 1998).

## Purposes of Assessment

We know that assessing students is murky business and yet, despite all the limitations, we persist with good cause. First and foremost, assessments can enable student agency within a teacher's curriculum—experts call this "assessment *for* learning" (Stiggins and Chappuis, 2012; Wiggins, 1998). Formative assessments, in particular, can provide a steady stream of data to help teachers adjust their instruction to meet their students' needs. For example, if students do not perform well on a particular task, it is incumbent upon the teacher to rethink what she is doing and respond to students' misconceptions.

Assessments also provide students with an opportunity to wrestle with ideas and to synthesize their learning. As students interact within a debate, unpack a historical document, construct a map, or create a demand and supply model, they externalize and refine their thinking about a topic. In other words, students can learn material by working through well-constructed assessments. Experts call this "assessment *as* learning" (Earl, 2012).

Teachers are also accountable for reporting the results of students' learning. It is simply unacceptable to tell parents or administrators that because there is no perfect assessment, we cannot actually tell them how students are doing in a particular class. Credentialing and certification are part of the educational enterprise and require teachers to ultimately provide "assessments *of* learning" (Wiggins, 1998).

Despite the challenges of knowing what students know, these purposes of assessment provide us with a call to do so. Because multiple purposes of assessment exist, we must be clear about why we are assessing and what kinds of instruments might help us best achieve our goals. In the following section, we describe the underlying principles that guide assessment opportunities and inform the *Tasks* within the IDM Blueprint design.

## The Nature of IDM Tasks

Central to the IDM tasks is Dewey's (1916) observation that students should be active within an inquiry: "Only by wrestling with the conditions of the problem at first hand, seeking and finding his own way out, does he think" (p. 33). The accumulating research evidence demonstrates the finding that students actively construct knowledge rather than passively receive it (Bruner, 1990; Grant, 2003; Newmann, Marks, and Gamoran, 1996; Piaget, 1962; Saye et al., 2013; Wineburg and Wilson, 1991).

The performance tasks threaded throughout the IDM are constructed to provide students with opportunities to learn by doing. We intentionally use the modifier *performance* for both formative and summative tasks to signal the idea that students are demonstrating their knowledge through application. Whether students are writing evidence-based claims or arguments, participating in a debate or structured discussion, or constructing a T-chart or Venn diagram, students are working "to demonstrate performance of certain skills or to create products that demonstrate mastery" (Stiggins and Chappuis, 2012, p. 138).

IDM performance tasks necessarily vary in their complexity, but each is designed to provide teachers with multiple opportunities to evaluate what students know and are able to do. In the early stages of an inquiry, students build knowledge through discrete but interdependent exercises that strengthen their capacity for success on the summative tasks. In the latter stages of inquiry, students work with more elaborated forms of communication that have real-world impact and consequence (Newmann et al., 1996). Taken together, these tasks allow students to build knowledge and to express their emergent understandings through a variety of means, but always with a meaningful purpose.

The C3 Inquiry Arc provides an organizational structure for IDM tasks that includes a strong emphasis on disciplinary knowledge and the structures of specific disciplines. At the same time, it recognizes that social studies students should have opportunities to apply disciplinary knowledge and skills as they examine enduring questions related to human experiences. In other words, the C3 Inquiry Arc roots disciplinary thinking (Dimension 2) within an interdisciplinary inquiry approach (Dimensions 1, 3, and 4).

Long debated in social studies circles, the question of whether to focus on content and conceptual knowledge or generic and disciplinary skills has been firmly answered in the *C3 Framework*: Good teaching focuses on both. Dimension 2—Applying Disciplinary Concepts and Tools—outlines the kind of disciplinary knowledge and skills students need to answer compelling questions. But skills and knowledge in isolation have little value (Lee, 2005). It is the application of skills in the pursuit of knowing and understanding the past and the present that defines the substance of social studies (Willingham, 2003). As students analyze sources in the completion of formative and summative tasks, they use the ways of thinking unique to social studies disciplines (e.g., civics, economic, geography, and history). The *C3 Framework* describes a range of disciplinary skills in Dimension 2 including using deliberative processes (civics), making economic decisions (economics), reasoning spatially (geography), and determining the purpose of a source (history).

Indications of the interaction between disciplinary knowledge and skills are represented in an inquiry through the IDM tasks. In these exercises, students demonstrate their content understandings and their abilities to apply one or more social studies skills as they engage with specific tasks. Students may be defining terms, identifying examples, and brainstorming ideas in the early part of an inquiry; they may be comparing similar and different instances of phenomena, analyzing text passages, and writing claims with evidence later on. The ability to synthesize the content developed throughout an inquiry and to express that synthesis in an evidence-based argument is key to successful completion of the summative performance task. Students need content in order to make an argument; they also need skills in order to craft and support that argument. Disciplinary knowledge and skills can be discussed independent of one another. Making and supporting arguments, however, demand that they interact.

In the following sections, we delve more deeply into the distinct but complimentary tasks within the IDM Blueprint. We begin with a discussion of summative performance tasks and the value that these tasks bring at the conclusion of an inquiry. Then, we move to the important role that formative performance tasks play in supporting students' content and skill development through the body of an inquiry.

## The Role of Summative Performance Tasks

The IDM features three types of summative performance tasks—arguments, extensions, and taking informed action—each intended to be a culminating experience of an inquiry. The summative argument is tied to an inquiry's compelling question and asks students to construct an evidence-based argument in response to it. Summative extensions and taking informed action tasks offer further opportunities for thoughtful exploration, creative expression, and civic participation. In the following sections, we outline the components of each of the three summative performance tasks types and explain their unique and collective value in preparing social studies students to be knowledgeable, thinking, and active citizens.

### Summative Argument Task

The summative argument task underscores the primacy of argumentation in the social studies (National Council for the Social Studies (NCSS), 2013; National Governors Association (NGA), 2010). That is, that while students engage in other forms of writing and thinking in their social studies classes, the ability to craft and defend an argument remains the centerpiece of a strong civic education:

> Anyone can ask a question about the social world and come to some answer or another, no matter how wildly speculative or opinionated. . . . A wildly speculative answer or an imaginative conjecture, however, is not the same thing as understanding. Understanding is achieved by the careful investigation of questions, data collection, reading, analysis, and synthesis; in effect, data are transformed into evidence-based claims that separate opinions and conjecture from justifiable understandings. (NCSS, 2013, p. 89)

The value of constructing evidence-based arguments that respond to a central question is seen consistently across inquiry models in the social studies (e.g., DBQ Project, the Big History Project, Beyond the Bubble) and is reinforced by the research done on teaching and learning in history education (see reviews by Barton, 2008; Grant, 2006; Lee, 2005; VanSledright and Limon, 2006). Pellegrino and Kilday (2013) observe that "in current history education scholarship, inquiry is characterized in part as 'doing' history where students develop and respond to queries about people, events and phenomena of the past through a cyclical process that engages primary and secondary sources to formulate evidence-based interpretations" (p. 4). In the IDM, we privilege argumentation as the chief outcome of an inquiry.

We define arguments as a collection of claims supported by relevant evidence that answer a researchable question (Grant, Lee, and Swan, 2015). The *C3 Framework* (NCSS, 2013) lays the foundation for the relationship between compelling questions and arguments within the backbone of the Inquiry Arc (Figure 3.1). In Dimension 1: Developing Questions and Planning Inquiries, students begin working with a compelling question by defining points of agreement and disagreement that emerge from the initial stages of an inquiry. In Dimension 4: Communicating Conclusions and Taking Informed Action, students construct arguments that respond to compelling questions and present summaries and adaptations of those arguments to a range of audiences both inside and outside the classroom through a variety of mediums.

Because of this important relationship between question and argument, we say that the blueprint is *convergent* around two structural points: the compelling question and the summative argument task. A convergent task is one where the activities have been sequenced and scaffolded in such a way that students' knowledge and skills *converge* in the construction of evidence-based arguments that respond to a compelling question. Although the IDM converges on an argument, that need not mean student arguments will all look the same. To the contrary, we would expect a wide range of arguments from students. In fact, we consider the capacity of a compelling question to result

**Figure 3.1** The C3 Inquiry Arc Shows the Relationship Between Compelling Questions and Summative Arguments

## IDM Follows C3 Inquiry Arc

If students are asked a **COMPELLING QUESTION**...

Students answer in the form of a **SUMMATIVE ARGUMENT**

in many different arguments as fundamental to inquiry design. For example, if students are asked to wrestle with a question like "Was the French Revolution successful?," they ultimately answer this question in the form of an evidence-based argument. Students could generate many versions of the following arguments: 1) The French Revolution *was* successful, 2) The French Revolution *was not* successful, or 3) The French Revolution *was* successful in some ways *and was not* in others. In this way, compelling questions are as functional as they are engaging and intellectually rich.

The IDM Blueprint hardwires in these two important elements by consistently highlighting the compelling question that launches the inquiry and the summative argument that brings the inquiry to resolution. To support this consistency across blueprints, we use a version of the following language in the summative argument task:

> Was the French Revolution successful? Construct an argument (e.g., detailed outline, poster, or essay) that addresses the compelling question using specific claims and relevant evidence and information from historical sources.

Three points are important here. First, we begin by reprinting the compelling question to signal that students are responding to the original question. Too often, we can lose track of our original instructional purpose when we engage in complex pedagogies like inquiry. The compelling question is constructed to engage students with a content and kid-friendly focus, but it is not ornamental. Instead, it is central to the inquiry, and students respond directly to the compelling question in the form of an argument.

Second, we consistently use the phrase "construct an argument" because arguments may take a number of forms—a five-paragraph essay, a chart, or a poster. The form in which an argument is expressed is less important than the opportunity it provides for teachers to see how their students express and defend their conclusions.

Third, students are expected to support their arguments with "specific claims and relevant evidence and information" from a range of disciplinary sources. It is important to note that each of the formative performance tasks and the summative performance tasks are source dependent. That is, students are working with a variety of disciplinary sources (e.g., maps, documents, diaries, newspaper articles) to develop their answers to either the supporting or compelling questions. In Chapter 4 of this book, we delve deeply into the nature of sources and the critical role they play within the blueprint.

The summative argument task changes slightly depending on grade level and inquiry focus. For example, although elementary-age students' facility with writing essays is limited, their ability to construct emerging arguments is not. Students in early grades can voice their perspectives and work by themselves and with others to develop their reasons for those perspectives. In doing so, even our youngest students can create arguments. For example, in a kindergarten-level inquiry on needs and wants, we use the following language for the summative argument task:

> Why can't we ever get everything we need *and* want? *In small groups*, construct arguments, supported with evidence, that address the question of whether or not we can ever get everything we need and want.

We still use the language of argument construction but create a purposeful scaffold, "in small groups," to suggest how teachers might structure the activity. We do not ask kindergarteners to create multiple claims or counterclaims, as we know their arguments will necessarily be less sophisticated than their 10th-grade peers.

To help students become more facile with the skills of argumentation, students need preparation in reading disciplinary sources, mining those sources for evidence, and building claims supported with evidence. Additionally, these exercises are not done in isolation but are anchored in the disciplinary content that will form the basis for their arguments. We address the important role that formative performance tasks play in preparing students for the summative argument task later in this chapter.

## Summative Extensions

Argument-based tasks are useful as direct measures of students' capacity to marshal evidence in support of their claims. Also useful, however, are *divergent* assessments, as they provide opportunities for teachers to stretch their students' understandings through more expressive modalities, including designing websites or wikis, creating digital documentary presentations, discussing and debating claims orally in the classroom, and engaging in writing collective essays (Hess, 2002; Klingner, Vaughn, and Schumm, 1998; Swan and Hofer, 2008; 2011; 2014). Each summative argument task, then, is paired with a summative extension task. These summative extensions can take many forms—a policy-writing activity, a documentary, a perspective-taking exercise. The idea is to present students with additional and alternative ways to engage with the ideas that are central to an inquiry.

In Dimension 4 of the *C3 Framework*, Communicating Conclusions and Taking Informed Action (NCSS, 2013), there is direction for adapting arguments to reach a range of audiences using multi-modal means:

> Having worked independently and collaboratively through the development of questions, the application of disciplinary knowledge and

concepts, and the gathering of sources and use of evidence and information, students formalize their arguments and explanations.

Products such as essays, reports, and multimedia presentations offer students opportunities to represent their ideas in a variety of forms and communicate their conclusions to a range of audiences. (p. 60)

The IDM recognizes the primacy of argumentation, but students truly come alive in social studies when they can creatively express their ideas in ways that impact others inside and outside the classroom. To ensure that students have a strong content foundation for the summative extensions, we foreground argumentation so that it is a staging ground for the meaningful tasks that follow.

In a French Revolution inquiry, students have an opportunity to use their arguments as a foundation for a perspective-taking exercise using the medium Twitter:

> Construct an imagined Twitter conversation among three historical figures: an **Enlightenment thinker** (e.g., Olympe de Gouges, Thomas Jefferson, John Locke,), **someone from the French Revolution** (e.g., Marie Antoinette, Napoleon Bonaparte, Georges Danton, Louis XVI, Toussaint L'Overture), **and an intelligent 10th grader living today** (e.g., yourself, someone in the class you admire and respect). The topic of the conversation is "Was the French Revolution successful?"

Within their Twitter conversations, students are asked to make coherent claims and to cite specific evidence from the sources analyzed within the inquiry as support.

Social studies educators rightly caution against using historical empathy exercises, as they can often lead to pure imagination, over-identification, or sympathy (Foster, 1999; Yeager and Foster, 2001). If constructed and staged properly, we believe that they can provide an engaging and meaningful opportunity for students. Before responding to the summative extension, students working through a French Revolution inquiry build a strong content foundation through the exercises within the formative performance tasks and by constructing the summative argument. Although there may be a degree of imaginary thinking in extension tasks, in this case, if students' tweets are grounded in the research done throughout the inquiry, then they are evidence-based. In this way, students are engaging "imagination restrained by evidence" (Davis, 2001, p. 3).

Because of their divergent nature, summative extensions vary widely across inquiries:

- ◆ In an early elementary inquiry on wants and needs, students can **create a two-sided collage** with images of needs (or goods) on one side and wants (or services) on the other.
- ◆ In an elementary-level inquiry on children's rights, students can express their arguments through a **class discussion using a "take a stand" protocol**.
- ◆ In a middle-school inquiry on *Uncle Tom's Cabin*, students can **create an educational video** of the arguments that responds to the compelling question "Can words lead to war?"

Extensions allow teachers to keep the summative tasks interesting and provide value beyond traditional school experiences (Newmann et al., 1996). In cases where teachers do an extension, they may want to consider modifying the summative argument to an outline, rather than a fully developed essay. However, it is important that an argument-building exercise come first to provide the intellectual foundation for a more creative extension.

## Taking Informed Action

Social studies has long been criticized for its limited attention to civic engagement (Campbell, Levinson, and Hess, 2012; Levine, 2007; Levinson, 2014). Learning how a bill becomes a law and how individual and group rights have been addressed by examining Supreme Court cases are useful activities. But if students' ideas and actions are confined to the classroom, then they miss important opportunities to see how those ideas and actions play out in other public venues. The IDM continues the *C3 Framework's* call to civic action by hardwiring this important social studies outcome into the heart of the blueprint.

Taking informed action tasks are designed so that students can civically engage with the content of an inquiry. Informed action can take numerous forms (e.g., discussions, debates, presentations) and can occur in a variety of contexts both inside and outside of the classroom. The key to any action, however, is the idea that it is informed. The IDM, therefore, stages the taking informed action activities such that students build their knowledge and understanding of an issue before engaging in any social action.

To that end, taking informed action can be described in three stages. In the *understand* stage, students demonstrate that they can think about the issues behind the inquiry in a new setting or context. The *assess* stage asks students to consider alternative perspectives, scenarios, or options as they begin to define a possible set of actions. And the *act* stage is where students decide if and how they will put into effect the results of their planning.

The understand-assess-act sequence of Taking Informed Action is articulated within Dimension 4 of the *C3 Framework*, Communicating Conclusions and Taking Informed Action. In the French Revolution inquiry, taking informed action follows this sequence:

- ◆ **UNDERSTAND:** Investigate a current "unfinished revolution" focusing on a group of people who are currently trying to revolutionize some aspect of society. This could be a political revolution or an economic, social, or even technological revolution.
- ◆ **ASSESS:** Examine the extent to which the current attempt at revolution is successful and state one's personal stance on the justification for the revolution or whether it is, in fact, a revolution.
- ◆ **ACT:** Write an editorial for the school or local newspaper on a current "unfinished revolution." Within the editorial, students could discuss their positions on the efforts of those engaged in revolutionary activity and the extent to which those efforts are currently successful.

Taking informed action tasks are included in each IDM Blueprint, but we acknowledge that teachers may not be able to enact the sequence due to time constraints. In some cases, taking informed action is embedded into the formative and summative performance tasks to ease the time burden on teachers and to make civic opportunities more seamless within the inquiry. For example, in a high school public policy inquiry on the Affordable Care Act (Table 3.1), understanding the problem is embedded into Formative Performance Tasks 1 and 2. Assessing the problem is embedded into Formative Performance Task 3 and 4. Acting on the problem serves as the summative extension of the argument. In this way, students have an opportunity to practice taking informed action within an inquiry rather than at the end.

Like summative extensions, taking informed action activities offer modularity to inquiry assessments. Although inquiries may end formally when students construct and support their arguments, teachers can vary the ways that students present those arguments by substituting the options represented in the extensions or the taking informed action activities.

**Table 3.1** Why Is the Affordable Care Act So Controversial?

| Supporting Question 1 | Supporting Question 2 | Supporting Question 3 | Supporting Question 4 |
|---|---|---|---|
| **Understand** | | **Assess** | |
| Who were the uninsured before the ACA? | How does the ACA work? | Why is the ACA a constitutional controversy? | Why is the ACA *still* controversial? |
| Formative Performance Task | Formative Performance Task | Formative Performance Task | Formative Performance Task |
| Create a graphic depiction of the uninsured before the ACA. | List key components of the ACA and write a paragraph summary of the goals of the ACA and the problems of the ACA. | Perform a reader's theater of *National Federation of Independent Business v. Sebelius* and write a paragraph majority opinion on the case or a paragraph dissenting opinion on the case. | Develop a claim about why the ACA is still controversial. |
| Summative Performance Task | ARGUMENT Why is the ACA so controversial? Construct an argument (e.g., detailed outline, poster, or essay) that addresses the compelling question using specific claims and relevant evidence and information from contemporary sources. | | |
| | ACT Create a student guide to the ACA that explains why 12th graders should care about this act. Within the guide, include a list of credible resources for learning more about the ACA. | | |

One of the most challenging parts of the *C3 Framework* and the IDM is taking informed action. A teacher's worst enemies are the clock and the calendar because, together, they limit time for teaching and learning. Additionally, teachers typically have not had much experience with action activities and may wonder if they are supposed to have students march on city hall. The good news is that there are many ways to take action and that teachers can help students do so right in the classroom.

Table 3.2 shows examples of action sequences that require a range of instructional time and student effort.

Although the understand-assess-action sequence is present in all three inquiries, the outcomes are quite different. Both the kindergarten and 11th-grade sequences can be done in the classroom within one to two class periods. The 7th-grade sequence asks students to work together to present

**Table 3.2** Examples of Taking Informed Action Sequences

| | In the Kindergarten inquiry on wants and needs, students can: | In the 7th grade inquiry on the Pilgrims and Wampanoag Indians, students can: | In the 11th grade inquiry on emancipation, students can: |
| --- | --- | --- | --- |
| **Understand** | Identify a need or want for the classroom. | Research the point of view of a modern indigenous group that is fighting for its rights. | Watch the film *Lincoln*. |
| **Assess** | Brainstorm methods of fulfilling the need or want for the classroom. | Explore whether or not conflict can be avoided in the situation you examined. | Using evidence generated from the inquiry as support, consider the extent to which the film accurately depicts the end of slavery. |
| **Act** | Select and act on a method of fulfilling the need or want for the classroom. | Create a video, Facebook page, or website that argues for or against the merits of the group's struggle and present the product at a classroom or community event. | Write a review of the film and post it to www.IMDB.com. |

to another classroom or community event, requiring a great deal of time and effort to organize.

## The Role of Formative Performance Tasks

For any summative task, students need preparation. Formative performance tasks act as a series of learning experiences that enable students to demonstrate their knowledge of the content, concepts, and skills that are needed to produce clear, coherent, and evidence-based arguments. The formative performance tasks reflect an inquiry's supporting questions and offer teachers snapshots of their students' progress so that they can modify their instructional plans if necessary.

### Formative Performance Tasks

The formative performance tasks within the IDM are designed not as activities but as *exercises* intended to move students toward success on the summative argument task. Students need experience with content and skills throughout an inquiry in order to make a strong argument. In this way, teachers avoid "gotcha" assessments—tasks that catch students off-guard or without the proper preparation for success on the summative performance tasks. Teachers should use data from these formative tasks to adjust their instruction and to improve student achievement on the summative performance tasks (see Black and William, 2009; Bloom, 1968; Popham, 1995). In the next section on evaluation, we talk about the role of these formative tasks as evaluative tools for instruction.

The IDM formative performance tasks are designed to include the major content ideas and disciplinary practices that provide the foundation for students' arguments. Dimensions 2 and 3 of the *C3 Framework* help provide clarity about the skills and conceptual knowledge that help to move students from question to argument. Using these skills and concepts, teachers can begin to structure the formative learning experiences that allow students to demonstrate their knowledge of the content, concepts, and skills needed to produce clear, coherent, and evidence-based summative arguments (Figure 3.2).

The formative performance tasks within IDM are framed by the supporting questions within the inquiry. Just as there is convergence between the compelling questions and summative argument task, there is congruence between a supporting question and the formative performance task. That is, the formative performance task is designed to measure students'

**Figure 3.2** The C3 Inquiry Arc Shows the Positioning of Formative Tasks Between Compelling Questions and the Summative Argument

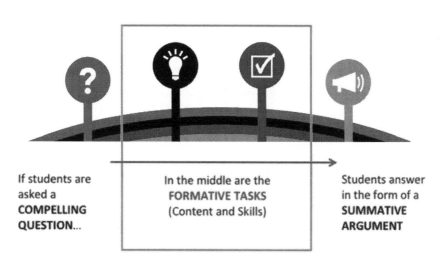

## IDM™ Follows C3 Inquiry Arc

If students are asked a **COMPELLING QUESTION**...

In the middle are the **FORMATIVE TASKS** (Content and Skills)

Students answer in the form of a **SUMMATIVE ARGUMENT**

understanding of the supporting question. Although compelling questions consistently converge on an argument, supporting questions can be answered in a variety of ways as long as the tasks are constructed to: 1) surface students' knowledge of the supporting question and 2) support students in constructing their arguments.

To examine these ideas further, let's return to an inquiry that features the compelling question, "Was the French Revolution successful?" In this inquiry, there are four supporting questions (SQ) and four formative performance tasks (FPT; Table 3.3).

Each of the formative performance tasks is designed to surface students' understanding of the content ideas identified in the supporting question. The major content ideas represented in the supporting question sequence include: 1) problems in prerevolutionary France, 2) early stages of the Revolution, 3) Robespierre and the Reign of Terror, and 4) Napoleon's rise to power. In each of the formative performance tasks, students have an opportunity to demonstrate their understandings of these key historical concepts.

If we zoom in on any one of the supporting questions and accompanying formative performance tasks, we can see more clearly the congruence between the two. For example, SQ1 reads, "What were the social, economic, and political problems in prerevolutionary France?" To demonstrate understanding

Table 3.3 Supporting Questions and Formative Performance Tasks in a French Revolution Inquiry

| Supporting Question 1 | Supporting Question 2 | Supporting Question 3 | Supporting Question 4 |
|---|---|---|---|
| What were the social, economic, and political problems in prerevolutionary France? | How did the relationship between the French people and the king change in the early stages of the Revolution? | How did Robespierre justify the Reign of Terror? | Did Napoleon's rise to power represent a continuation of or an end to revolutionary ideals? |
| **Formative Performance Task** | **Formative Performance Task** | **Formative Performance Task** | **Formative Performance Task** |
| List **social, economic, and political problems in prerevolutionary France.** | Write one or two paragraphs explaining how **the relationship between the French people and the king changed between 1789 and 1793.** | Write a summary of **Robespierre's justification for the Reign of Terror** and identify two key details that support his justification. | Develop a claim supported by evidence about whether **Napoleon's rise to power** represents a continuation of or an end to revolutionary ideals. |

of this question, students "list social, economic, and political problems in prerevolutionary France." Teachers use students' responses to the task to evaluate whether or not they are ready to proceed to the next formative performance task. If there is misalignment between the task and the question, it will be unclear whether students have acquired the necessary skills and knowledge to be successful on the summative argument.

The second role of the formative performance tasks is to support students in constructing their arguments. In this way, the formative performance tasks converge on the summative argument. To make an evidence-based argument about the success or failings of the French Revolution, students need practice with a variety of discrete skills including analyzing sources, understanding multiple perspectives, and making claims with evidence. The formative performance tasks within an inquiry allow students to practice these types of analytical and argumentation skills while they work through the important content ideas of an inquiry. For example, in the French Revolution inquiry, the four formative performance tasks allow students to acquire the foundational content knowledge of the Revolution and to practice the skills required within the summative performance task:

- *List* social, economic, and political problems in prerevolutionary France.
- *Write one or two paragraphs* explaining how the relationship between the French people and the king changed between 1789 and 1793.
- *Write a summary* of Robespierre's justification for the Reign of Terror and *identify two key details* that support his justification.
- *Develop a claim supported by evidence* about whether Napoleon's rise to power represents a continuation of or an end to revolutionary ideals.

Within this sequence of tasks, students practice a variety of skills (e.g., reading and evaluating disciplinary sources, writing paragraphs supported by details from sources, and developing claims with evidence) that move them progressively toward argument construction.

It is important to note that these formative performance tasks build in complexity across the IDM Blueprint. In the French Revolution inquiry, students begin with a relatively straightforward task of listing problems in prerevolutionary France and then move to the more advanced work of developing evidence-based claims about Napoleon's rise to power. In other inquiries, we see this increasing complexity as well.

Let's return to the Kindergarten needs and wants inquiry and examine the formative performance task construction for SQ-FPT congruence, FPT-Summative Argument convergence, and this increasingly complex task progression (Table 3.4).

**Table 3.4** Supporting Questions and Formative Performance Tasks in a Needs and Wants Inquiry

| Supporting Question 1 | Supporting Question 2 | Supporting Question 3 |
|---|---|---|
| What do we want? What do we need? | How do goods and services meet our needs and wants? | What happens when there isn't enough for everyone? |
| **Formative Performance Task** | **Formative Performance Task** | **Formative Performance Task** |
| Sort and categorize items as **needs or wants**. | Identify a **need or want** and determine ways in which it could be satisfied through **goods and services**. | Participate in a discussion of options people have when faced with **scarcity**. |

The major content ideas that undergird the supporting questions are reflected in the formative performance tasks. As we discussed in the last chapter, students begin with the foundational economic concepts of needs and wants. Then, students are asked to think about these needs and wants and how they can be satisfied with two additional concepts, goods and services. Finally, students work with all four concepts (wants, needs, goods, and services) through the concept of scarcity in a real-world setting. The progression of intellectual complexity that is inherent within the supporting questions is necessarily present in the formative performance tasks as the tasks measure students' understanding of the inquiry concepts.

As students work with more complex content ideas, they are asked to demonstrate their understanding in more complex ways. Students begin in the first formative performance task by defining needs and wants through an exercise of sorting and categorizing. To do so, students use an image bank and sort the images into a T-Chart labeled "wants and needs" (Figure 3.3).

**Figure 3.3** Image Bank for an Inquiry on Needs and Wants

**Figure 3.4** Formative Performance Task for an Inquiry on Needs and Wants

| Draw a picture of a *good* related to food. | Draw a picture of a *service* related to food. |
|---|---|
| I could get this by | I could get this by |
| _____ | _____ |
| _____ | _____ |
| _____ | _____ |
| _____ | _____ |

Then, in the second formative performance task, students illustrate one good and one service related to food and one good and one service related to school. Students use these illustrations to determine a means by which they might acquire each of those goods and services. See Figure 3.4.

Finally, in the third formative performance task, students participate in a discussion about ways to manage scarcity—the condition of not being able to have all the goods and services that a person needs or wants. The formative performance task calls on students to engage in a discussion about a scenario based around scarcity:

> The Weather Channel predicts that there will be a snowstorm tonight. On your way home from school, your family decides to stop at the grocery store to pick up a few items they need in case it does snow.

Through small group discussions, students brainstorm options people have when faced with scarcity and share their ideas with the class. In doing so, students are moving purposefully toward the summative argument in which they respond to the compelling question, "Why can't we ever get everything we need *and* want?" In this way, students move through a progression of increasingly complex tasks—definition to application to analysis.

Researchers like Bloom (1956) and Webb (1997) have tried to capture this idea of increasing task complexity by creating leveled categories of expertise. In the IDM, we create neither a single language nor do we prescribe a particular taxonomy around the progression of tasks. Rather, we suggest that the blueprint should contain a pedagogical rationale for the sequence and composition of the formative tasks that prepare students for the summative performance tasks.

## Staging the Compelling Question

Staging the Compelling Question tasks are actually the first, and perhaps the most important, formative experiences that students encounter within the IDM. These tasks are constructed to hook students into the inquiry through a 15–20 minute activity that sparks their interest. Although compelling questions are constructed to be kid-friendly, even the very best questions may need to be introduced so that students are excited to explore them and understand the inquiry focus.

Just how to generate curiosity is, in large part, a pedagogical issue. The IDM approach recognizes the important role sources can plan in helping students become interested in knowing more about an inquiry topic. For example, in a French Revolution inquiry, we acknowledge that students may not understand the relevance of this historic revolution on its face so we begin the inquiry with a look at a modern-day revolution in Egypt. Students in this inquiry could examine the initial stages of the 2011–2013 Egyptian revolution alongside its unintended consequences by looking at the news and photograph documentation easily available on the Internet.

From this more contemporary revolution, a skilled teacher can help students recognize that revolutions are relevant in today's world and that history, although a study of the past, has important implications for the world in which they live. Also, she can use this revolution to teach that shifts often occur during revolutions, that they can create unforeseen consequences, and that radical political and social change is often messy.

In the examples in Table 3.5, we see these opportunities as a way of getting to the enduring ideas within an inquiry.

**Table 3.5**

| Inquiry Grade and Topic | Compelling Question | Staging the Compelling Question |
| --- | --- | --- |
| 1st grade<br>Global Citizen | Why should I be a global citizen? | Watch a video on changing the world and brainstorm the meaning of the term **"citizen."** |
| 7th grade<br>*Uncle Tom's Cabin* | Can words lead to war? | Consider the **power of words** and examine a *video* of students using words to try to bring about positive change. |
| 10th grade<br>Modernization | Does development mean progress? | Read the *UN description of the Human Development Index (HDI)* and examine the United States HDI rank. Discuss what students think **"development"** and **"progress"** mean. Students could also read an *NPR blog post* and discuss the costs and benefits of labeling countries as "developing." |

In each of these examples, the Staging the Compelling Question exercise pulls on an important concept within the inquiry (e.g., citizenship, power of words, development and progress) and anchors the task with an engaging disciplinary source (e.g., a video, the Human Development Index, NPR blog post). In doing so, the IDM acknowledges both the importance of affective as well as intellectual engagement within inquiry.

\* \* \* \* \*

The *C3 Framework* sounds an important alarm for social studies educators:

> Now more than ever, students need the intellectual power to recognize societal problems; ask good questions and develop robust investigations into them; consider possible solutions and consequences; separate evidence-based claims from parochial opinions; and communicate and act upon what they learn. (p. 91)

IDM tasks provide curricular spaces for students to practice communicating and acting upon what they have learned. In essence, they are *doing* social studies rather than passively learning about it. The summative performance tasks are intended as academic and civic crescendos to inquiry, but they also provide a rationale for engaging with the formative work that comes before. As the research literature suggests, too often we ask students to ingest conclusions, rather than to form their own (Brophy and Alleman, 2008; Cuban, 1991).

By contrast, enabling students to form their own conclusions is the bedrock of the IDM. In doing so, we invite students to become active sense makers who "wrestle with problems and find their own way out" (Dewey, 1916, p. 33).

## Evaluation of IDM Tasks

The IDM Blueprint includes a range of formative and summative performance tasks that can be used for a variety of evaluative purposes. As we noted in the beginning of this chapter, performance tasks can be designed for different assessment purposes—tasks *for* learning, *as* learning, and *of* learning. Therefore, we largely stay silent on the evaluation of student work, honoring a teacher's best judgment for how these tasks serve her instructional purpose. Although argument tasks may be formal opportunities for summative judgment about a student's ability, they can also be a formative checkpoint preceding a summative extension. In either case, a teacher would need to decide how to treat each task according to its purpose within an inquiry or within a larger unit of study.

Evaluating students' work also involves knowing the abilities of a particular group of students. When providing feedback to students, teachers consider many variables, including a student's experience with a task. Any criteria deemed "proficient" would be quite different for a novice than for a more practiced student. Clearly, a student who is constructing a claim for the first time should have different expectations than those of a student who is more experienced with the task. Any performance task will elicit a range of student responses according to their facility with language, understanding of the content, and engagement with the material. We chose not to build generic rubrics for the IDM tasks, as it would be impossible to take all of this variability into account.

When developing performance criteria, experts suggest that teachers should define the attribute(s) being evaluated and develop a continuum of performance (Airasian, 1991; Popham, 1995; Stiggins, 1994). For example, if students are making a digital documentary, an attribute might be "using visual effects" and the extent to which the use of images enhances the film's narrative (Swan and Hofer, 2014). As for the performance dimension, proficiency could range from "advanced" (e.g., use of images enriches the film's narrative) to "developing" (e.g., use of images is tangential to film's narrative). Ultimately, each formal assessment should have performance criteria attached to it so that students have clear expectations and teachers become consistent in their feedback across students and over time (Wiggins, 1998).

Teachers clearly need to think about the evidence of learning that they collect, how they evaluate student work, and the ways that student work informs their own instruction. They also should consider the time and energy it takes to provide meaningful feedback and to consider strategies to make evaluation more efficient. The IDM tasks are constructed to ease the burden of evaluation in two ways. First, the tasks are typically concise. A response to a formative performance task that asks students to develop a claim supported by evidence could take the following form:

> Napoleon directly challenged the democratic ideals of the *Declaration of the Rights of Man and Citizen*, 1789, by reinstating the divine right of the emperor.
>
> The French people, by a free and independent expression, then manifested its desire that the imperial dignity should pass down in a direct line through the legitimate or adopted descendants of Napoleon Bonaparte, or through the legitimate descendants of Joseph Bonaparte, or of Louis Bonaparte.
>
> **Source A**: Excerpts from Napoleon's account of the internal situation of France, 1804

Second, IDM tasks work together and build to a final learning experience. As students work through the formative tasks, they are progressing to one or more summative performance tasks that purposefully embed the work that has come before. Teachers could consider thinking about all of the tasks within an inquiry more holistically, rather than as discrete assignments. In doing so, the work of the inquiry could be evaluated as a whole, rather than the sum of its parts.

## Moving Forward With Sources

As an instructional framework, IDM builds out from the C3 Inquiry Arc: 1) compelling and supporting **questions** that frame and give structure to the inquiry (Dimension 1); 2) summative and formative performance **tasks** that provide the opportunities for communicating conclusions (Dimension 4). Disciplinary **sources** allow students to explore the compelling question, build content expertise, and develop the disciplinary skills to successfully support and defend their ideas (Dimensions 2 and 3). IDM features sources across the blueprint, but sources are most prominently associated with the formative performance tasks. In this way, they represent the building blocks of inquiry. In this next chapter, we take a close look at both the nature and function of disciplinary sources within the IDM.

# 4

# Sources *Are* the Matter

Sources are central to the success of inquiry. Sources deliver content, encourage disciplinary thinking, and even inspire students to want to learn more. Sources give rise to questions, inform learning tasks, and ultimately provide students evidence in support of an argument.

Sources are relevant across the full scope of the Inquiry Arc, but they are also full of contradictions and complications. We have to keep in mind the original purpose of sources. A letter to a friend, a record of a transaction, or a photograph of an event, each of these was created for some purpose, a purpose that was unique in time and in the place where it was created. In an inquiry, we change the way we think of sources, shifting their original purpose to the service of teaching and learning. That letter to a friend, in this context, is not just a personal interaction; it becomes something more—potential evidence to support a claim. The same is true with an official record of a transaction or a photograph of an event. In an inquiry, all sources have their original intent, which is something that students must understand, but more importantly, sources contain information that is ultimately useful in making an argument.

How we use the word *source* matters as well. Sources are things. They have a material substance—a book, a map, an official record, an artifact—all can be seen and held, and in some cases even smelled or tasted. Sources are also the material of an inquiry. Sources have intellectual value in helping students complete formative and summative tasks as they answer compelling and supporting questions. Sources provide the content students need to accomplish learning goals and to solve problems. But sources are far from obvious. They rarely, if ever, directly convey the information students need in an inquiry. Instead, sources require a process for appropriating information from the source to suit our needs in an inquiry. Sources are so dependent on process, we even use the verb *sourcing* to convey an element of the activity required to use sources. For our purposes, a source *is any material that can be useful in an inquiry toward the goal of answering questions.* Sources hold within information that can function as evidence in making claims, which when stitched together take form as arguments. Driven by questions and structured with tasks, sources provide the substance of an inquiry. In sum, sources are the materials that help students construct arguments in response questions.

Two questions drive this chapter: What role do sources play in the Inquiry Design Model and, more specifically, how can teachers support students as they use sources in an inquiry? In this chapter, we examine the role of sources in an inquiry and in the IDM, the instructional uses of sources, and the ways that teachers prepare sources for use in an inquiry. Along the way, we consider examples of sources. But first we give some consideration to the role of sources in an inquiry.

## Sources and Inquiry

Sources serve three important purposes in the Inquiry Design Model. They help to initiate and spark inquiry, they provide students with the background knowledge they need to sustain an inquiry, and they supply the evidence needed to support arguments at the conclusion of an inquiry. In several ways, sources enable teachers and students to accomplish the goals of inquiry and the *C3 Framework*. Across the Inquiry Arc of the *C3 Framework*, sources play a role when teachers and students pose questions and plan inquiry (Dimension 1), when they engage the tools and concepts of the discipline (Dimension 2), when they evaluate sources and use evidence (Dimension 3), and when they communicate conclusions and take informed action (Dimension 4). Sources are important in all aspects of the *C3 Framework*'s Inquiry Arc and the Inquiry Design Model (Figure 4.1). Using the IDM, teachers can create opportunities for students to work with sources across all four dimensions of the C3 Inquiry Arc so that they can produce a clear, coherent, and evidence-based argument.

Our interest in highlighting sources in the Inquiry Design Model follows decades of research and practice, particularly in the discipline of history (Barton, 1997; Hartzler-Miller, 2001; Hicks, Doolittle, and Lee, 2004; Holt, 1990; Levstik, 1996; VanSledright, 2002a; Wineburg, 1991; Yeager and Davis, 1996). Sources are central to the disciplines that make up social studies, but they also play a critical role in writing and argumentation (Monte-Sano and

**Figure 4.1** Sources in IDM and the Inquiry Arc

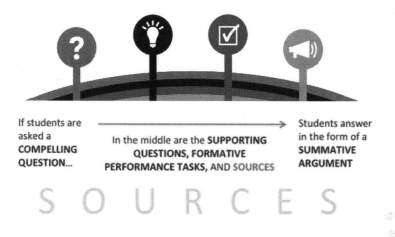

De La Paz, 2012). Sources are also now being used regularly to support Common Core implementation (Newman, Degener, and Wu, 2015).

Today, a dizzying number of sources are available online from a vast number of providers, many of these at no cost to teachers and students. Online repositories abound, but two of the most comprehensive collections can be found at the Library of Congress (www.loc.gov) and the National Archives and Records Administration (www.archives.gov). Access to such an amazing variety of disciplinary sources is changing the way we can and should teach social studies. Direct access to original writings, maps, political cartoons, artwork, and the like offers terrific opportunities for students to experience inquiry.

Not all sources are cut from the same cloth, however. Many sources are textual—diaries, newspapers, histories—but not all. Sources can be graphic (e.g., artwork, posters, documentaries); they can be spatial (e.g., maps) and have physical properties (e.g., artifacts). Some sources may even be embodied in people (e.g., oral interviews). Understanding the diverse and situated nature of sources, the IDM takes a measured and consistent approach to using sources in an inquiry. In the Inquiry Design Model, sources function to help students respond to compelling and supporting questions and to complete tasks that deepen their content knowledge and provide opportunities to practice with the skills of the social studies disciplines. Thus far we have been inclusive in thinking about how sources broadly work in an inquiry. We have argued that any source, in virtually any form, that helps students complete inquiry tasks and answer inquiry questions is useful. However, we also recognize that social studies is composed of academic disciplines, so we have an obligation to also teach students the tools and habits of mind of the disciplines. Such work can be accomplished through inquiry and an emphasis on the disciplinary nature of sources.

## The Disciplinary Nature of Sources

In our definition of sources, we describe them as being useful in answering inquiry questions and such sources often originate in the social studies disciplines. The origins of a source are important because we believe strongly that sources provide students with access to the subject matter they need to complete formative tasks in an inquiry, make arguments in response to compelling questions, and ultimately to live and act in our civic world. But sources are not a quick fix for student ennui. Barton (2005) cautions against the use of primary sources in ways that may communicate "misconceptions" about the disciplines (p. 746). We have to guard against using sources as a replacement for lectures and textbooks. Using sources to simply convey subject matter is likely no better than a steady diet of lecture. At the same time, the notion that disciplinary sources have some magical power to transform social studies into a scaled-down version of what political scientists, or economists, or geographers, or historians do is equally problematic.

Perhaps the most recognizable feature of sources is the distinction, made most often in history, between primary and secondary sources. Primary sources are those materials closest to the topic being studied, and secondary sources are typically produced from the study of primary sources. This distinction is quite useful when describing how sources function in an inquiry, but teachers should be cautious not to overuse it as a way to categorize sources (Barton, 2005). By themselves, primary sources have limited value. Primary sources are not able to "tell" a story. To the contrary, secondary source are interpretations. The intention of a secondary source is to explain.

The key function of sources in an inquiry is that they provide students with information. Whether explicitly or implicitly, sources offer ideas and information about human experiences. Some sources, such as textbooks or secondary historical accounts, convey information directly. These secondary sources are designed to explain and describe. Primary sources are typically less direct in how they convey information. When working with primary sources in an inquiry, students are changing the original intent of the source; the depth of cognitive engagement required of students when working with sources follows suit, with primary sources requiring an expert type of analysis (Levstik and

Barton, 2015). However, the way in which sources are situated in an inquiry—the demands of the tasks—impact how sources are actually used by students.

For example, a high school inquiry might ask the question, "Does it matter who freed the slaves?" To answer that question, students analyze both primary and secondary sources. They use three primary sources, including parts of the 1861 and 1862 Confiscation Acts, the 1863 Emancipation Proclamation, and 1865 Thirteenth Amendment, to annotate a timeline. To complete this task, students pull information directly from these primary sources with little analysis. In contrast, the other sources in this inquiry represent excerpts from essays written by historians Ira Berlin and James McPherson—a couple of classic secondary sources. As students work with these secondary sources, they create a T-chart that contrasts arguments that Lincoln freed the slaves to arguments that the slaves freed themselves. The information from these secondary sources is in dynamic tension, requiring that students understand the strengths and weaknesses of both arguments and make judgments about the relative value of each. This task requires more analytical effort on the part of students than the timeline task.

Inquiry challenges children to think beyond their comfort zone, and work with sources is quite possibly the most uncomfortable of all the work students will do in an inquiry. Students need scaffolds and guidance to be successful in this complex work, a type of direction that blends the capacity of sources to convey information and their capacity to yield evidence with a healthy dose of the disciplinary tools to support students as they analyze those sources (Ashby, 2011; Counsell, 2000; Jordanova, 2000). This is just what Dimension 2 of the *C3 Framework* (NCSS, 2013) aims to do by representing the concepts and tools of the disciplines:

> Sources come in many forms, including historical and contemporary documents, data from direct observation, graphics, economic statistics, maps, legislative actions, objects, and court rulings. Access to these and other digital sources is now more readily available than ever. The availability of source materials, however, does not translate automatically into their wise use. Students must be mindful that not all sources are equal in value and use and that sources do not, by themselves, constitute evidence. Rather, evidence consists of the material students select to support claims and counter-claims in order to construct accounts, explanations, and arguments. (p. 18)

Work with sources requires much from students, and the crux of this work is a process of transforming information in sources and putting that information to work as evidence. Rosalyn Ashby (2011) explains, "Sources yield evidence but only when they are used as such, to support a claim, back up a theory, establish a fact or to generate a hypothesis" (p. 140). However, it's not just that sources contain potential evidence as Counsell (2011) reminds us:

> The question or enquiry we are pursuing determines how we might use any given source as evidence. It is not possible to determine the value, usefulness, utility or reliability of a source, or its category as primary or secondary, independently of the use to which we want to put it as evidence. (p. 141)

Sources contain potential, and that potential is realized when students use skills to develop knowledge. Disciplinary knowledge and skills are integrated within an inquiry and take form as students examine sources. Opportunities for students to apply disciplinary knowledge and skills when working with sources run throughout an inquiry but are most obvious in the IDM formative and summative tasks. In those exercises, students demonstrate the intersection of their content understandings and their ability to apply one or more social studies skills as they engage with the specific tasks. As we learned in Chapter 3, those tasks build in intellectual and skill sophistication as the formative performance tasks unfold. Students may be defining terms, identifying examples, and brainstorming ideas in the early part of an inquiry; later, they may be comparing similar and different instances of a phenomenon, analyzing text passages, and writing claims with evidence. The ability to synthesize the content developed throughout an inquiry and to express that synthesis in an evidence-based argument is key to successful completion of the summative performance task.

## Types of Disciplinary Sources

Social studies disciplines feature ways of thinking about sources that are useful when trying to understand how they can be used. For example:

- ◆ Legislation and government policies are particularly useful in **civics**; thus public policies evaluation is important.
- ◆ Data sets and statistics are common in **economics**; thus quantitative reasoning is important.
- ◆ Maps and GIS data are representative of **geography**; thus spatial reasoning is important.
- ◆ Oral history and diaries are typical sources in **history**; thus perspective determination is important.

The *C3 Framework* includes a "Disciplinary Inquiry Matrix," offering examples of how experts in the disciplines might inquire about the compelling question—"How bad was the recent Great Recession?" The sources suggested for addressing the question illuminate how sources within the disciplines are uniquely positioned in relation to the question:

Civics: Government policies, policy pronouncements, political poll results, statistics, leadership efforts, political behavior; observations of local conditions, interviews; news reports

Economics: Statistics and lots of them in as real time as possible (labor, capital, credit, monetary flow, supply, demand)

Geography: Spatial and environmental data; statistics, map representations, GIS data to measure observable changes to the planet; indicators of territorial impact

History: Accounts from the recent recession and from hard economic times in the past, both firsthand and synthetic, as many as can be found (oral history, diaries, journals, newspapers, photos, economic data, artifacts, etc.)

Because disciplines are organized as they are and are interested in particular questions about human activities, specific kinds of sources are typical within disciplines. Thus, sources have unique value within an academic discipline. Returning to our example from the *Uncle Tom's Cabin* inquiry, a wide range of disciplinary sources might be useful to address the compelling question, "Can words lead to war?"

◆ In political science, the Fugitive Slave Act might be a useful source.
◆ In economics, data on cotton exports could be useful.
◆ In geography, a useful source might be a map of the United States that highlights the number of enslaved persons.
◆ In history, the writings from New York abolitionist Gerrit Smith may be helpful.

These sources are useful from a disciplinary perspective because they enable students to use concepts and approaches commonly employed within the academic disciplines that make up social studies. Such disciplinary uses of sources are described in Dimension 2 of the *C3 Framework* and are embedded in the performance tasks found in inquiries created using IDM. As an approach to designing instruction, IDM also offers some specific instructional uses of sources. In the next section, we review these instructional uses of sources.

## Sources in the Inquiry Design Model

Given the disciplinary nature and instructional uses of sources, how do sources actually work in the IDM? In this section, we begin to examine this issue by thinking about the relationship between sources, questions, and tasks.

### The Relationship Between Sources and Questions

When designing inquiries that follow the IDM approach, teachers will find that the fit between the questions and sources is critically important. Sources must provide students with opportunities to successfully respond to compelling and supporting questions as they complete formative and summative tasks. In an upper-elementary inquiry on the Declaration of Independence, students examine the text in the Declaration of Independence in response to the compelling question, "Why do countries declare independence?" (Table 4.1). The supporting questions for this inquiry align directly with three parts of the Declaration. In fact, the first three supporting questions were written with these three parts of the document in mind. The fourth supporting question asks about other declarations of independence in the Western Hemisphere and features summary level source material, but teachers may choose to include other sources such as excerpts from other declarations

**Table 4.1** Why Do Countries Declare Independence? Questions and Sources in an Inquiry

| Supporting Question 1 | Supporting Question 2 | Supporting Question 3 | Supporting Question 4 |
|---|---|---|---|
| What are the two big philosophical ideas in the Declaration of Independence? | What grievances did the colonists have with King George III? | How does the Declaration of Independence make an argument for independence? | How do declarations of independence from other countries in the Western Hemisphere compare with the United States Declaration of Independence? |
| **Featured Sources** | **Featured Sources** | **Featured Sources** | **Featured Sources** |
| **Source A:** Part 1 of the Declaration of Independence: Preamble | **Source A:** Part 2 of the Declaration of Independence: Grievances | **Source A:** Part 3 of the Declaration of Independence: Conclusion | **Source A:** Table of independence declarations in Latin America<br><br>**Source B:** Source packets: Declarations of independence material for Haiti, Venezuela, and Mexico |

of independence in the Western Hemisphere. This inquiry highlights the dynamic relationship between supporting questions and sources where the supporting question may lead to specific sources or may require that teachers think more broadly about possible sources.

A middle-level inquiry on the Great Compromise makes clear how sources can be flexible. The inquiry asks the compelling question, "Is compromise always fair?" As students work toward an argument in the summative performance task, they respond to four supporting questions:

◆ How was representation determined under the Articles of Confederation?
◆ What was the Virginia Plan?
◆ What was the New Jersey Plan?
◆ How did the Connecticut Plan break the impasse?

Carefully selected sources provide students opportunities to access the content suggested by these questions (Table 4.2).

**Table 4.2** Is Compromise Always Fair? Questions and Sources in an Inquiry

| Supporting Question 1 | Supporting Question 2 | Supporting Question 3 | Supporting Question 4 |
|---|---|---|---|
| How was representation determined under the Articles of Confederation? | What was the Virginia Plan? | What was the New Jersey Plan? | How did the Connecticut Plan break the impasse? |
| **Featured Sources** | **Featured Sources** | **Featured Sources** | **Featured Sources** |
| **Source A**: Excerpt from Articles of Confederation | **Source A**: Excerpt from *Notes of Debates in the Federal Convention of 1787* (Virginia Plan) <br><br> **Source B**: Diagram of the Virginia Plan <br><br> **Source C**: Chart of the US population in 1790 | **Source A**: Excerpt from *Notes of Debates in the Federal Convention of 1787* (New Jersey Plan) <br><br> **Source B**: Diagram of the New Jersey Plan | **Source A**: Excerpt from *Notes of Debates in the Federal Convention of 1787* (Introduction to the Connecticut Plan) <br><br> **Source B**: Excerpt from *Notes of Debates in the Federal Convention of 1787* (Virginia and New Jersey Plans) <br><br> **Source C**: Excerpt from *Notes of Debates in the Federal Convention of 1787* (Approval of the Connecticut Plan) |

The first supporting question asks students to describe congressional representation under the Article of Confederation. Students are provided with an excerpt from Article V of the Articles of Confederation. The excerpt includes very specific information about representation. Although the supporting question appears to be fairly straightforward, teachers may go in different directions. For example, if a teacher is just interested in students understanding the number of representatives from each state, then they would make use of the information highlighted here:

> For the more convenient management of the general interests of the United States, delegates shall be annually appointed in such manner as the legislature of each state shall direct, to meet in Congress on the first Monday in November, in every year, with a power reserved to each state to recall its delegates, or any of them, at any time within the year, and to send others in their stead, for the remainder of the Year.
>
> No State shall be represented in Congress by less than two, nor by more than seven Members; and no person shall be capable of being delegate for more than three years, in any term of six years; nor shall any person, being a delegate, be capable of holding any office under the United States, for which he, or another for his benefit receives any salary, fees or emolument of any kind.

If the teacher wants, in addition or instead, to focus on how states manage their delegates in Congress, then they would focus on a different part, such as the following text:

> For the more convenient management of the general interests of the United States, delegates shall be annually appointed in such manner as the legislature of each state shall direct, to meet in Congress on the first Monday in November, in every year, with a power reserved to each state to recall its delegates, or any of them, at any time within the year, and to send others in their stead, for the remainder of the Year.
>
> . . .
>
> Each State shall maintain its own delegates in a meeting of the states, and while they act as members of the committee of the states.

In the IDM, questions and sources are just part of the larger instructional design. Tasks provide students with the impetus to and structure for responding to questions through the analysis of sources.

## The Relationship Between Sources and Tasks

As we have seen, sources align closely with questions in the IDM, and since
tasks are similarly derived from questions, the relationship between sources
and tasks is also close. All formative and summative tasks are anchored by
sources, and students' experiences with and abilities to respond to the tasks
will largely be shaped by their work with the sources. The task structure in
the Inquiry Design Model provides a path for students to gather information from sources and construct knowledge in formative and summative
ways. Sources provide students with the content they need to complete tasks,
develop content knowledge, and practice disciplinary skills.

Returning to the inquiry on the Great Compromise, it is clear how sources
provide students an opportunity to complete tasks (Table 4.3). As students

**Table 4.3** Is Compromise Always Fair? Sources and Tasks

| Supporting Question 1 | Supporting Question 2 | Supporting Question 3 | Supporting Question 4 |
|---|---|---|---|
| How was representation determined under the Articles of Confederation? | What was the Virginia Plan? | What was the New Jersey Plan? | How did the Connecticut Plan break the impasse? |
| **Formative Performance Task** | **Formative Performance Task** | **Formative Performance Task** | **Formative Performance Task** |
| Write a description of how states were represented in the Congress under the Articles of Confederation. | Write a summary of the Virginia Plan highlighting the impact on large and small states. | Write a summary of the New Jersey Plan highlighting the impact on large and small states. | Write a claim with evidence about how the Connecticut Plan broke the gridlock at the Constitutional Convention. |
| **Featured Sources** | **Featured Sources** | **Featured Sources** | **Featured Sources** |
| **Source A**: Excerpt from Articles of Confederation | **Source A**: Excerpt from *Notes of Debates in the Federal Convention of 1787* (Virginia Plan)<br><br>**Source B**: Diagram of the Virginia Plan<br><br>**Source C**: Chart of the US population in 1790 | **Source A**: Excerpt from *Notes of Debates in the Federal Convention of 1787* (New Jersey Plan)<br><br>**Source B**: Diagram of the New Jersey Plan | **Source A**: Excerpt from *Notes of Debates in the Federal Convention of 1787* (Introduction of the Connecticut Plan)<br><br>**Source B:** Excerpt from *Notes of Debates in the Federal Convention of 1787* (Virginia and New Jersey Plans)<br><br>**Source C:** Excerpt from *Notes of Debates in the Federal Convention of 1787* (Approval of the Connecticut Plan) |

work toward the summative task and an argument in response to the compelling question, "Is compromise always fair?," they complete four formative performance tasks.

Each task is completed through students' analysis of sources. In the inquiry on the Great Compromise, those tasks range from writing a description of representation in Congress under the Articles of Confederation to writing summaries of the Virginia and New Jersey plans. The tasks build toward the fourth formative performance task, where students write a claim with evidence about how the Connecticut Plan broke the gridlock at the Constitutional Convention. Here students will need to put their skills to work at the highest level. To complete this fourth task, students are provided with three sources, all excerpts from James Madison's notes on the Constitutional Convention. The first of these three sources describes Elbridge Gerry's Connecticut Plan. The second is a recounting of James Wilson's comparison of the Virginia and New Jersey Plans. The third and final excerpt is a recording of the votes on the Connecticut Plan. Each source includes extensive annotations to help students access the information they may use as evidence to support their claims. In making those claims, students would need to think about how the Connecticut Plan broke new ground, what made the plan different than the two previous plans from Virginia and New Jersey, and how the plan appealed to states in both the north and the south.

The relationship between sources, questions, and tasks is important, but perhaps more important are the implications of these connections. Let's now look more closely at these implications by focusing on the instructional uses teachers may make of sources in an inquiry.

## Instructional Uses of Sources

The Inquiry Design Model is clear about the relationship between sources and tasks and provides a means by which teachers can use sources to help students develop knowledge and practice skills from the social studies disciplines. But what about the actual instructional moves that teachers must make to pull off an inquiry? IDM provides a general structure for conducting inquiry, but most of the instructional decisions about how the inquiry will be implemented remain in the hands of teachers. No model can replace a skilled teacher who understands her students' needs and the unique contexts driving instruction in the classroom. However, IDM is certainly not silent on all instructional questions. The Inquiry Design Model suggests three instructional uses of sources:

◆ to spark curiosity to initiate and sustain an inquiry
◆ to build disciplinary (content and conceptual) knowledge through the use of disciplinary skills
◆ to construct arguments with evidence.

**Table 4.4** Instructional Uses of Sources and IDM Blueprint Tasks

| Instructional uses of sources | Relevant to IDM Blueprint tasks |
|---|---|
| Sparking curiosity | • Staging the compelling question<br>• Formative performance tasks<br>• Taking informed action |
| Building disciplinary knowledge | • Formative performance tasks<br>• Summative argument tasks<br>• Summative extension<br>• Taking informed action |
| Constructing an argument | • Summative argument tasks<br>• Summative extension |

In this section, we explore these three instructional uses of sources and describe how each of these instructional uses of sources comes to life through various tasks of the IDM Blueprint (Table 4.4).

## Sparking Curiosity With Sources

Sparking curiosity is about engaging students as they initiate and sustain an inquiry. Just how to generate curiosity is, in large part, a pedagogical issue. In the IDM, sources play an important role in helping students become curious and interested in knowing more about an inquiry topic. The use of sources to spark curiosity is closely connected with compelling questions. After all, one of the defining features of a compelling question is the question's capacity to reflect one or more of the qualities or conditions that we know children care about.

Sources in the Staging the Compelling Question task can be useful in helping to spark curiosity. Sources may continue to inspire and nurture curiosity throughout an inquiry, whether as a boost along the way or as a way to move an inquiry in a new direction. Sources can help spark curiosity in a number of ways. Some sources might *disrupt* how students think about the topic at hand. Other sources might *intrigue* students. Still other sources might be *recognizable* to students but are being framed by a question or activity that asks students to think about them in a new way. The idea is for the source to draw students into the inquiry as a whole or into some task or aspect of the inquiry.

Social studies teachers have long used pedagogical strategies such as our staging exercises. Madeline Hunter (1982) described these strategies as an anticipatory set that prepares students to begin the process of developing new knowledge. In the IDM, we put these long-held practices to work as part of a larger effort to support inquiry learning and disciplinary thinking. In the inquiry on *Uncle Tom's Cabin*, we use a video created by eighth-grade students to do just that. The video draws students into the inquiry and provides them with an initial experience that will hopefully capture their attention and enable them to make personal connections. The video is described in the inquiry as follows:

> This video on Kailash Satyarthi, produced by seventh-grade New York State students, was the third-place winner of the Speak Truth To Power video contest, which encourages middle and high school students to become engaged in human rights through video production. Students are asked to choose a human rights issue and an activist identified by Robert F. Kennedy Human Rights and then create a three- to five-minute video that creatively discusses the issue/activist and any local connections that might exist. Students also reflect on the larger lessons the activist's life can teach us and how we can all make a difference with the chosen issue.

This video source enables students to think about the power of words as they begin an inquiry on the compelling question, "Can words lead to war?" The video demonstrates some of all three of the qualities of sparking curiosity outlined earlier (disruptive, intriguing, and recognizable). The source deals with the topic of child labor and, for many students, will disrupt the way they think about childhood. It should be intriguing for students given that 8th grade students created the video. The video should also be recognizable in that it was produced using a form that is ubiquitous in students' social and academic life today.

Sources can be used across an inquiry to spark curiosity as well. A secondary-level inquiry on Civil Rights asks the question, "What made non-violent protest effective during the civil rights movement?" This inquiry includes a featured source intended to support students as they complete the first formative task:

> Featured Source B is a 22-minute theatrical presentation about the Greensboro sit-in created by the Smithsonian's National Museum of American History. This video simulation, called Join the Student Sit-Ins, happens at the museum, where a portion of the actual lunch counter from the protest is on display (see a picture at the Object of History website: http://objectofhistory.org/objects/intro/lunchcounter/). The video features an African American student, Samuel Leonard (a fictional composite character), who is conducting a training session for people interested in joining the 1960 sit-in protests against racial segregation.

When students encounter this source, they will be well into the inquiry. This source may serve to jump-start or extend students' curiosity as they move into the formative tasks. The video provides students with an opportunity to engage with content about the techniques used in the sit-in movement, but it does that in an interesting way that is likely to appeal to students.

## Building Knowledge With Sources

As a comprehensive approach to teaching and learning, inquiry helps students do many things, but perhaps most importantly inquiry helps students build knowledge. With a solid knowledge base in place, teachers and students can take on all of the summative tasks that are possible with IDM—arguments, extensions, and taking informed action. But, we have to begin somewhere—students must start with knowledge of something.

In their seminal work on the science of learning, Bransford, Brown, and Cocking (1999) argue that inquiry learning demands factual knowledge coupled with conceptual understandings and a useful learning process:

> To develop competence in an area of inquiry, students must: (a) have a deep foundation of factual knowledge, (b) understand facts and ideas in the context of a conceptual framework, and (c) organize knowledge in ways that facilitate retrieval and application. (p. 1)

The IDM puts forward a way to organize knowledge and develop new knowledge that is heavily dependent on factual and conceptual knowledge. But, it's not just that facts serve as the stuff of an inquiry. More importantly, such content knowledge helps children learn more. As Willingham (2009) argues, "When it comes to knowledge, those who have more gain more" (p. 44). The IDM provides students with scaffolded processes to carefully encounter facts and other content using conceptual knowledge to build on what they already know.

In the IDM, disciplinary sources are the "source" of information and ultimately knowledge. Students develop knowledge as they work with sources to complete tasks in the service of compelling and supporting questions. IDM contrasts with non-inquiry approaches where the sources of knowledge are more directly accessible, and oftentimes directly delivered by teachers through lecture and direct instruction. Teachers who embrace IDM cede some control over the process of students constructing knowledge. Instead of teachers delivering interpretations from sources, students are actually doing the analysis themselves. That means students may go in different directions with their interpretations and thus with their arguments. But, what teachers might lose in controlling the flow of information, they gain in student agency and the depth of knowledge being developed by students.

For students to successfully build their knowledge, sources within an inquiry must convey information. The illustration in Figure 4.2 is a source for the first formative performance task in the inquiry on *Uncle Tom's Cabin*. It conveys content by providing a powerful visual representation of an important episode in the book. In this illustration, Eliza comes to tell Uncle Tom and his wife, Chloe, that Eliza's son, Harry, and Tom have been sold to a slave trader. Eliza had just overheard the news from her master, Mr. Shelby, that the trader will arrive in the morning to take Tom and Harry away. In a panic, Eliza plans that night to run away. The illustration and other sources related to the task (another illustration and four text passages) collectively enable students to know more about how Harriet Beecher Stowe described slavery through the fictionalized experiences of the characters in the book.

A common question asked of IDM is how does it differ from other approaches to developing knowledge. Why not lecture, or use a textbook or even a movie? The IDM approach to knowledge building is unique because it enables students to use disciplinary skills to build their knowledge. IDM places considerable cognitive demand on students to construct knowledge in ways that are similar to how we work in the disciplines. This approach does not negate the occasional more direct approaches to building knowledge. To the contrary, by using IDM as a part of a larger set of instructional approaches, teachers are able to provide differentiated instruction. Importantly, students must have a wide range of learning experiences that enable them to work

**Figure 4.2** Illustration From the First Edition of *Uncle Tom's Cabin*

with their knowledge and apply their conceptual understandings in the many ways that we must work with knowledge in college, career, and civic life.

Using disciplinary sources to build knowledge in an inquiry is not easy work. Students must draw upon their conceptual understandings and apply disciplinary skills when working with sources to build knowledge. The nature of the source often determines the type of disciplinary skills that are needed. Building knowledge using a map requires a specialized set of spatial reasoning skills. The better grasp that students have of geographic concepts, the better able they are to create new geographic knowledge. Using economic data demands other conceptual understandings and another skill set. Historical sources demand still other concepts and skills. These disciplinary concepts and skills are reflective of the ways of thinking within social studies disciplines: civics, economics, geography, and history. At the same time, students need to develop more generic inquiry skills such as gathering information from sources, interpreting information given relevant contexts, determining the biases of sources, or using information from sources as evidence to support claims.

Ultimately, students are trying to gather information from the source for the purpose of completing tasks. As students gather information from sources during an inquiry, they are building up a storehouse of knowledge. Developing a deep reservoir of knowledge is one of the advantages of inquiry. Another advantage with inquiry is that students are processing information in response to thoughtful questions and thus developing their knowledge in more practical ways (Newmann and Wehlage, 1993). Adding to this advantage is the task-based structure of IDM that enables students to work with all of this knowledge in ways that learning scientists argue lead to better retention (Rosenshine, 2012). This surplus of knowledge, deeper engagement, and longer retention pays off when students are expected to recall discrete pieces of information on quizzes and tests and when they are assessed using longer and more disciplinary forms.

## Constructing Arguments With Sources

Inquiry crescendos with the construction of arguments, and students' capacity to construct arguments is a fundamental goal of the *C3 Framework* and a key feature in the IDM. Sources play an important role in the construction of arguments. Arguments take form as a coherent collection of claims supported by evidence, and the evidence for claims and counterclaims is contained within sources.

Pulling information from sources can be difficult for students, so teachers need to provide students with support across the formative performance tasks as they build a storehouse of information that might be used as evidence.

Monte-Sano (2012) describes five indicators of how students use evidence for written arguments in social studies:

◆ Factual and interpretive accuracy
◆ Persuasiveness of evidence
◆ Sourcing of evidence
◆ Corroboration of evidence
◆ Contextualization of evidence

Three of these indicators—sourcing, corroboration, and contextualization—derive from Wineburg's (1991) seminal work examining the differences between novice and experts analyzing historical documents. These three indicators represent disciplinary ways of thinking. The other two indicators—factual and interpretative accuracy and persuasiveness—point to the ways in which the argument is composed.

Strategies to support students as they analyze sources to meet the five indicators described by Monte-Sano (2012) are a good starting place. The formative performance tasks might also include some practice with making claims and using evidence, so that the summative argument is not the first time students have considered how to use the information emerging in the inquiry as evidence. But, it is important to remember that not everything students learn in an inquiry will make it into an argument.

Each of the sources in an inquiry holds the potential to contribute in unique ways to an argument. For example, in the *Uncle Tom's Cabin* inquiry, these two sources play an important role in developing an argument around the compelling question, "Can words lead to war?"

◆ In the **Letter from Harriet Beecher Stowe to Lord Thomas Denman, 1853,** Stowe describes her feelings about abolitionism. From this source and her concluding remarks in the book, students can determine Stowe's motivation for writing *Uncle Tom's Cabin*. By examining Stowe's motivation, students gather information about how abolitionism was a powerful force in the lives of people like Stowe and the recipient of the letter, Lord Thomas Denman.
◆ The source on **Sales of *Uncle Tom's Cabin*** is useful as evidence in establishing the popularity of *Uncle Tom's Cabin*. Using this source, students might make an inference that the popularity of this book, as an anti-slavery work, reflected a larger abolitionist sentiment in the country. This information, combined with other information from sources, can be used as evidence for students to make claims about the impact of the book.

The summative performance task in the IDM calls on students to construct and support arguments, and sources play a big role in that process. Throughout an inquiry, students examine sources through a carefully designed sequence of formative performance tasks in order to develop the knowledge they need to make claims with supporting evidence. As students become more sophisticated in making arguments, they should begin to include evidence-based counterclaims that acknowledge other sides of an argument. All of this is complicated work, requiring teachers to support their novice students to make rather sophisticated intellectual judgments.

Now, let's shift gears to explore some specific ways that teachers can support students when working with sources.

## Teachers Supporting Students Working With Sources

Source work is complex. In an inquiry, students are being asked to complete tasks that are quite sophisticated, and students are mostly novice when it comes to those tasks (Beck and Jeffrey, 2009; Brett, and Thomas, 2014; De La Paz, and Felton, 2010). To support students as they take on these complex tasks and move toward developing more expert-like ways of thinking, we think it is important for teachers to make three additional considerations when using sources in an inquiry:

- ◆ Selecting sources
- ◆ Scaffolding
- ◆ Adapting sources

### Selecting Sources in an Inquiry

The selection of sources for an inquiry and their presentation to students are important considerations. Since sources serve as the primary means by which students encounter disciplinary knowledge (content and concepts), great care should be taken in selecting sources.

Perhaps more than another other aspect of the Inquiry Design Model, the number and scope of sources will impact the implementation of the inquiry, specifically with regard to timing. Generally speaking, the more sources and the longer the sources, the more time it will take to complete the inquiry. For this reason, we use the term "featured sources" in the IDM. These featured sources are among many that might be included in an inquiry, but were selected in recognition that working with sources takes time, something teachers don't always have a lot of. The use of the term "featured sources" also signals teacher agency and control in the implementation of the inquiry.

The feature sources are suggestive of sources that teachers might use in an inquiry, but are not prescriptive or limiting in terms of how the inquiry might actually be taught.

Selecting sources is a part of the inquiry design process that has considerable pedagogical overtones. To be successful in the process of selecting sources, teachers must be very knowledgeable of the inquiry topic. But even with exhaustive knowledge of content, there is no single stockpile of or perfect place to go in order to get sources. Unlike prepackaged resources such as textbooks, disciplinary sources in an inquiry can be found in lots of different places. A helpful place to look for sources is in collections assembled by disciplinary experts in libraries, archives, and other scholarly outlets. Many of the sources that teachers need for inquiries can be found online in digital archives. Collaborative efforts to share sources among teachers are an important part of the process of building up collections. In our work, we have taken on this ethos of sharing by adopting an open-source approach to publishing inquiries.

Examining the decisions behind the selection of sources for a supporting question in the *Uncle Tom's Cabin* helps to illuminate the process. For this supporting question—How did Harriet Beecher Stowe describe slavery in *Uncle Tom's Cabin*?—sources include a summary of *Uncle Tom's Cabin*, four excerpts from the book, and two illustrations:

- ◆ Featured Source A, the summary, was found at the Harriet Beecher Stowe Center—www.harrietbeecherstowecenter.org/utc/. In selecting this source, the authors of the inquiry were looking for a brief, authoritative, and readable summary of the book.
- ◆ Featured Source B includes excerpts from *Uncle Tom's Cabin*. The excerpts were taken from a version of the book available on Project Gutenberg at www.gutenberg.org/files/203/203-h/203-h.htm#link2HCH0030. The passages focus on Stowe's descriptions of slavery, which represents the supporting question.
- ◆ Featured Source C includes two illustrations from the first edition of the book and were found in an online project available at the University of Virginia and developed by Professor Stephen Railton at http://utc.iath.Virginia.edu/uncletom/illustra/52illf.html. These illustrations extend and punctuate the text passages and provide students with a different modality through which to learn about Stowe's depiction of slavery.

Selecting sources is just the beginning of the process when designing an inquiry. After the sources have been determined, teachers much think about how to adapt those sources given knowledge of their students.

## Adapting Sources in an Inquiry

It is rare that a source, as created, is perfectly suited for use in an inquiry. Because most of the sources in inquiries are being placed into duty as interpretative materials for students, changes to the sources are often necessary. Some sources, such as photographs, may be used "as is" in an inquiry, but most sources require adaptation (Wineburg and Martin, 2009). This process of adapting sources for use in an inquiry can take three forms: excerpting, modifying, and annotating.

One of the more common means of adapting sources is through excerpting. When making an excerpt, teachers select portions of a source that will be useful in an inquiry. These selections must contain enough information to be useful in the inquiry, but not so much as overwhelm the inquiry process. The excerpt also needs to be faithful to the original. If the excerpt doesn't include enough information to help students know what the source is, then an annotation might be needed. Making just the right selection requires deep knowledge on the part of teachers and likely will take a lot of time. Collaboration among teachers where they share source excerpts can help to mitigate some of those burdens. Monte-Sano (2012) describes a process for supporting students as they use sources as including "excerpts from primary sources" along with "secondary sources that can be used to support the arguments highlighted by the primary sources" (p. 295).

As a second potential adaptation, the modification of sources is often required. Some sources may be difficult for students to read or view. In such cases, teachers modify the source by inserting definitions or changing words in the text. Some may object to making changes to sources; they argue that changing sources does more harm than good. When considering this point, teachers should keep in mind the purpose of the source in the inquiry and ask themselves whether they are using the source for the source's sake or to accomplish some other learning goal. It is probably rare that sources would need to be used just for the sake of using the original source. With good sources having been selected and consideration for how to adapt those sources, teachers must then turn to the support needed for students' work with sources.

Even with carefully selected excerpts and modifications, some students may need annotations of the sources or additional descriptions. Annotations can frame the context of a source or provide more information about content suggested within the source. Teachers may want to use annotations to provide more information about the maker, date, place of origin, intended audience, and purpose. Some sources (e.g., photographs, drawing, maps) may need an annotation because of the type of source.

Recognizing that these sources were not made with teachers' and students' purposes in mind, Monte-Sano (2012) is willing to use "abbreviated documents, altered vocabulary, and removed potentially distracting elements"

(p. 295). Teachers need to think about the forms in which they present sources to their students. Although there is considerable value in reading sources in their original length and language, there are also advantages to excerpting, modifying, and/or annotating sources, especially long and conceptually dense texts. Sources ought to provide students with an opportunity to engage with content, not a barrier to that content.

Some sources may require two or three of these adaptations. This is most often true of difficult sources that include challenging content and/or language, as can be seen in this example of the adaptation of a source in an inquiry built around the compelling question, "Did the Chinese and Romans know each other?" (See Figure 4.3.)

This source from the Chinese historian Yu Huan was written almost 1800 years ago and has been translated from its original ancient Chinese. Even with this modern translation, the source contains difficult words and ideas. To provide students with an opportunity to access relevant information from the source, we carefully selected an 89-word excerpt. Given the potentially

**Figure 4.3** Example of Annotating, Modifying, and Excerpting

## Supporting Question 2

| Featured Source | **Source D:** Yu Huan, description of Romans, *Weilue* or *Brief History of the Wei* (excerpts), 265 CE |
| --- | --- |

*NOTE: Weilue, or the brief history of the Wei, was written by Yu Huan. Wei or Cao Wei was one of three states in that vied for power in the Three States Period of Chinese dynastic history (220-280 CE). In this passage Yu Huan draws on several sources to describe Romans.*

Annotation

This country (the Roman Empire) has more than four hundred smaller cities and towns. It extends several thousand li in all directions. The king has his capital (that is, the city of Rome) close to the mouth of a river (the Tiber). The outer walls of the city are made of stone.

...The ruler of this country is not permanent. When disasters result from unusual phenomena, they unceremoniously replace him, installing a virtuous man as king, and release the old king, who does not dare show resentment.

The common people are tall and virtuous like the Chinese, but wear hu ('Western') clothes. They say they originally came from China, but left it.                Modification

They have always wanted to communicate with China but, Anxi (Parthia), jealous of their profits, would not allow them to pass (through to China).

From *China Meets the West: The "Peoples of the West" During the 3rd Century CE According to the Weilue* (forthcoming). © John Hill. 2015.

Excerpt

difficult context of this source, we added an annotation. We also made a few modifications to help students develop a larger understanding of the source.

### Scaffolding Source Work in an Inquiry

Scaffolds provide students with support as they complete complex tasks. The IDM encourages complex performance tasks and thus requires the thoughtful use of scaffolds. Such scaffolds can take many forms from "hard," or very specific and repeatable forms of support, to "soft," or less specific ways to support students' work with sources (Brush and Saye, 2002). Soft scaffolds are dynamic and context-dependent. For example, teachers may ask students simple comprehension questions as they read excerpts from *Uncle Tom's Cabin* to support (e.g., Who is the author?). Soft scaffolds often emerge based on the needs of students in specific learning circumstances and are rarely used in prescribed ways.

Hard scaffolds are more fixed in their nature. Hard scaffolds may be used in a variety of learning contexts to support students as they engage in more general tasks. Such hard scaffolds can be teacher-created or they may emerge from research and have broad applications. For example, the SCIM-C approach to analyzing historical sources offers a repeating five-phase approach where students summarize, contextualize, infer, monitor, and corroborate, given a historical inquiry question (www.historicalinquiry.com).

In the Inquiry Design Model, teachers can make use of a wide range of borrowed and original scaffolds that draw on research and teacher knowledge about what works when students analyze sources. Ultimately, these scaffolds provide students with support in practicing generic literacy skills and more specific disciplinary skills as they move from novice-like thinking to more expert ways of thinking. Source work is demanding—it's sophisticated literacy work—and thus requires considerable support in the form of scaffolds.

## Sources and Literacy

We intuitively know that inquiry in social studies involves the use of sophisticated literacy skills; after all, when we ask and answer questions, we typically read and write and speak and listen. The *Common Core English Language Arts* standards provide a foundation for inquiry in social studies through its emphasis on reading rich informational texts, writing evidence-based arguments, and speaking and listening in public venues. These foundational literacy skills support the pedagogical directions advocated in the *C3 Framework* (Lee and Swan, 2013). The task-based structure of IDM requires that students read and write regularly. Building on foundational literacy skills, the IDM enables students to develop unique inquiry and disciplinary literacies (Lee and Swan, 2013).

Drawing on indicators in Dimensions 1, 3, and 4 of the *C3 Framework*, the task-driven structure of IDM supports 13 specific C3 inquiry literacies:

- ◆ Questioning
- ◆ Selecting sources
- ◆ Gathering information from sources
- ◆ Evaluating sources
- ◆ Making claims
- ◆ Using evidence
- ◆ Constructing arguments and explanations
- ◆ Presenting arguments and explanations
- ◆ Critiquing arguments and explanations
- ◆ Adapting arguments and explanations
- ◆ Analyzing social problems
- ◆ Assessing options for action
- ◆ Taking informed action

In addition to foundational and inquiry literacies, IDM encourages disciplinary literacies. These disciplinary literacies are the specific literacy skills students need to understand, create, and communicate academic knowledge (Shanahan and Shanahan, 2008). As students analyze sources when completing formative and summative tasks in an inquiry, they use the ways of thinking unique to social studies disciplines (e.g., civics, economics, geography, and history). The *C3 Framework* describes these disciplinary literacies in Dimension 2 as including skills such as using deliberative processes (civics), making economic decisions (economics), reasoning spatially (geography), and determining the purpose of a source (history).

Sources round out the Inquiry Design Model. With compelling and supporting questions in place and a series of tasks that challenge students to think about the content suggested by those questions, sources provide students with the subject matter for work. Sources *are* the matter. In this book, we have laid out an approach to thinking about inquiry that we think holds great potential for centering teaching and learning in social studies on practices common to the disciplines that make up social studies. But, more importantly, we see the Inquiry Design Model as putting forward an approach to social studies that brings social studies in sharp focus as an indispensable subject in school. IDM makes it clear that social studies matters.

# Conclusion

We know that inquiry isn't new or easy. Scholars across the disciplines have explicitly advocated for inquiry and inquiry-based practices since the early twentieth century (Dewey, 1902). Over the past 100 years, social studies researchers have chronicled the benefits and challenges of inquiry-based practices (Grant, 2003; Grant and Gradwell, 2010; Yeager and Davis Jr., 2005), and curriculum developers have created a raft of tools and resources to help teachers envision and enact inquiry experiences in social studies classrooms (Brown, 1996; Dow, 1970; Saye and Brush, 2005, 2006; Swan et. al., 2008). And, yet, inquiry as the defining element of classrooms remains as elusive as ever.

Drawing on decades of research, the *C3 Framework* (NCSS, 2013) provided an opportunity to posit a structure for social studies inquiry and to articulate a common language for inquiry experiences through the construction of the Inquiry Arc. The Inquiry Arc is composed of four distinct but interlocking dimensions: 1) developing questions and planning inquiries; 2) applying disciplinary concepts and tools; 3) evaluating sources and using evidence; and 4) communicating conclusions and taking informed action. The Inquiry Design Model (IDM) instantiates each of the four dimensions of the Inquiry Arc (Grant et al., 2015; Lee et al., 2015; Swan et al., 2015) into a curriculum and instructional model that operationalizes inquiry for social studies teachers.

Questions open an inquiry in the IDM and initiate the Inquiry Arc. Tasks animate IDM and provide opportunities for students to use disciplinary concepts and tools as they evaluate sources using evidence to communicate conclusions and take informed action. Sources make inquiry possible and are evidenced across all four dimensions of the Inquiry Arc.

These three elements reflect a long tradition of inquiry in social studies, much of it captured in the work around history education. There, the Amherst Project (Brown, 1996), Historical Scene Investigations (Swan et al., 2008), and Problem-Based Historical Inquiry (Brush and Saye, 2014) efforts have promoted the deep study of important questions through the use of disciplinary sources and a range of formative and summative tasks. The Stanford History Education Group is extending that work in both curricular and assessment directions (http://sheg.stanford.edu). Building inquiry across a wider curriculum scope are early efforts like "Man: A Course of Study" (Dow, 1991) and current work around Authentic Intellectual Work (Saye and Associates, 2015).

We believe that the focus of the IDM around the foundational elements of inquiry offers teachers an anchor for making inquiry more visible and for achieving the ambitions of the *C3 Framework*. Through those ambitions, teachers can create social studies experiences that "support students as they develop the capacity to know, analyze, explain, and argue about interdisciplinary challenges in our social world" and enable them to "communicate and act upon what they learn" (National Council for the Social Studies, 2013, p. 6).

## Constructing Inquiry

Questions, tasks, and sources are the foundational elements of inquiry. The Inquiry Design Model (IDM) provides a structure so that each element is distinct but interdependent—an electrifying compelling question will not matter if students are not tasked with answering it. Formative assignments and source work can be seen as pedantic if students do not understand what part they play in answering a meaningful question. In other words, any segment of the blueprint could be seen as a collection of busy work activities if the interaction of the elements is not apparent.

The one-page IDM Blueprint (see Table 5.1) provides teachers with a visual snapshot of the compelling and supporting *questions* that frame and organize an inquiry, the assessment *tasks* that provide opportunities for students to demonstrate and apply their understanding, and the disciplinary *sources* that allow students to practice disciplinary thinking and reasoning. Most importantly, the blueprint is not laden down with pages of instructional prescriptions; thus teachers can focus on the uniqueness of each element— questions, tasks, and sources—and the way they build together toward a coherent purpose.

In the following sections, we review and summarize the role and importance of each element and how they interact within the blueprint.

**Table 5.1** Inquiry Design Model (IDM) Blueprint™

| Compelling Question | | |
|---|---|---|
| Standards and Practices | | |
| Staging the Question | | |
| **Supporting Question 1** | **Supporting Question 2** | **Supporting Question 3** |
| | | |
| **Formative Performance Task** | **Formative Performance Task** | **Formative Performance Task** |
| | | |
| **Featured Sources** | **Featured Sources** | **Featured Sources** |
| | | |
| Summative Performance Task | **Argument** | |
| | **Extension** | |
| Taking Informed Action | | |

## Questions

The Inquiry Design Model (IDM) features compelling questions as a way to drive social studies inquiry. Answers are important, but a well-framed question can excite the mind and give real and genuine meaning to the study of any social issue.

The key to crafting compelling questions is hitting the sweet spot between the qualities of being intellectually rigorous and personally relevant to students. Intellectually rigorous questions reflect an enduring issue, concern, or debate in social studies and speak to the big ideas of history and the social sciences. An intellectually rigorous question is also representative of the content in standards and curriculum and reflects what educators and the communities invested in schools deem worth learning about. Compelling questions need to be worth investigating from an academic angle, but they also need to be worth exploring from a student perspective. To take this point seriously does not mean that we have to dumb down the curriculum. In fact, it means just the opposite: Teachers *should* teach intellectually ambitious material. The key is to see within the ideas to be taught those elements about which teachers know their students care.

It is not the case that students are uninterested in elections, economic down-turns, historic conflicts, and social movements. But it is the case that teachers need to pull relevant connections from those ideas to students' lives.

If compelling questions frame an inquiry, supporting questions sustain it. Supporting questions build out the compelling question by organizing and sequencing the main ideas. Supporting questions follow a content progression that becomes increasingly more sophisticated over the inquiry experience.

Taken together, the compelling question and supporting questions provide the content and conceptual scaffolding for the inquiry as they highlight the ideas and issues with which teachers and students can engage.

## Tasks

The Inquiry Design Model (IDM) features a variety of performance tasks that provide students with opportunities for learning and teachers with opportunities to understand and assess what students know and are able to do. Based on the idea that assessments serve instructional as well as evaluative purposes, the IDM features both formative and summative performance tasks as well as extension activities and taking informed action opportunities.

IDM begins with a compelling question that is consistently answered in the form of an argument. To produce clear, coherent, and evidence-based arguments, students need preparation. The formative performance tasks within the inquiry are designed as exercises intended to move students toward success on the summative task. Although these tasks do not include all of what students might need to know, they do include the major ideas that provide a foundation for their arguments and an opportunity to practice the skills of crafting and supporting arguments. Building on the purpose and structure of the summative and formative performance tasks, extension exercises highlight the alternative ways in which students may express their arguments. Such activities are in keeping with Dimension 4 of the *C3 Framework*, which asks students to 1) present adaptations of their arguments, 2) do so with a range of audiences, and 3) do so in a variety of venues outside of the classroom.

Finally, taking informed action experiences are designed so that students can civically engage with the content of an inquiry. Informed action can take numerous forms (e.g., discussions, debates, presentations) and can occur in a variety of contexts both inside and outside of the classroom. The key to any action, however, is the idea that it is informed. The IDM, therefore, stages the taking informed action activities such that students build their knowledge and understanding of an issue before engaging in any social action.

The instructional approach of the IDM is to employ a range of both forma-tive and summative performance tasks that provide students an opportunity to actively construct knowledge that will help them express their responses to compelling questions in meaningful ways.

## Sources

With compelling and supporting questions in place, along with a series of formative and summative performance tasks, sources complete the Inquiry Design Model (IDM). Sources provide the substance for an inquiry.

Because there are far more sources on every topic than could be listed in the inquiries and because no one source can address every aspect and perspective on that topic, the IDM takes the approach that some sources should be featured. To that end, sources in an IDM inquiry support three instructional purposes: 1) sparking and sustaining student curiosity in an inquiry, 2) building students' disciplinary knowledge and skills, and 3) enabling students to construct arguments with evidence. These three uses of sources directly support the performance tasks within the IDM Blueprint.

It is rare that a source, as created, will be perfectly suited for use in an inquiry; changes to the sources are often necessary. Some sources, such as photographs, may be used as is in an inquiry, but many sources require adaptation in one of three ways:

- ◆ Excerpting—using a portion of the source for the inquiry. Care should be taken to preserve information in the source that students may need to know about the creator and context of the source.
- ◆ Modifying—inserting definitions and/or changing the language of a text. Modifying texts increases the accessibility of sources.
- ◆ Annotating—adding short descriptions or explanations. Annotations allow teachers to set a background context for sources.

Source work adds texture and dimension to the blueprint. Sources animate the inquiry with material from the disciplines—information on our civic lives; data about economics; spatial representations of the places we interact; voices from the past and present—all working in concert to provide the interpretative matter through which students can think through and answer a compelling question.

## Bringing It All Together

The Inquiry Design Model (IDM) takes intellectual and affective engagement as its general starting point. A compelling question serves to initiate an inquiry; a summative performance task, where students address that question, serves to pull the inquiry together. The beginning and end points are important, but no more so than the components—supporting questions, formative performance tasks, and sources—that compose the middle of the Inquiry Design Model.

The blueprint reflects a conscious decision not to produce fully developed and comprehensive curriculum units or modules. Teachers should find considerable guidance within each inquiry around the key components of instructional design—questions, tasks, and sources. What they will not find is a complete set of prescriptive lesson plans. Experience suggests that teachers teach best the material that they mold around their particular students' needs and the contexts in which they teach. Rather than scripts reflecting generic teaching and learning situations, the IDM encourages teachers to draw on their own wealth of teaching experience as they adjust questions, tasks, and sources to transform the inquiries into their own, individual pedagogical plans.

Our hope is that the IDM signals to teachers a very important message: Inquiries require one's expertise and individual craft to fully come to life. One of the teacher leaders on the NY Toolkit project, Steve Lazar, summarized the strength of the IDM approach in the following blog excerpt from C3Teachers.org:

> These inquiries are in many ways unlike any other curriculum product I've seen. While publishers often brag about "teacher-proof" curriculum, I have often joshed that these inquiries are "administration-proof." They cannot simply be handed to a teacher who is told to do them. There is no scripting. These are in many ways minimalist sketches of a sequence of lessons that demand adaptation and decision-making by thoughtful, professional teachers.

To underscore this point, we share inquiries with an open invitation to remix and fit the inquiries to meet teachers' needs. Teaching with inquiry is necessarily a public act. To support teachers, we created an educator network called C3Teachers.org (http://c3teachers.org). C3Teachers aims to empower teachers as they wrestle with the big ideas and instructional implications of the *C3 Framework* in general and inquiry in particular. Teachers play a critical role in helping students learn academic content using the inquiry. As social studies as they design their own inquiries, C3Teachers aims to support teachers as they examine and experiment with their own practices and encourage students to question, learn, apply, analyze, collaborate, express, and act in authentic social studies experiences. C3teachers.org is a place to learn more about the inquiry process and to share experiences with other social studies teachers. Inquiries are available on C3Teachers in both PDF and Word documents so that teachers are encouraged to adapt and improve the inquiries for their particular contexts. Our belief is that inquiries should reflect a teacher's unique instructional practice and the needs and interests of their students.

## Looking Ahead

We know from our own successful and failed experiences that inquiry is far from easy. This book lays an important theoretical foundation for the Inquiry Design Model (IDM), but our work is just starting.

Our commitment going forward is to continue mining the Inquiry Design Model so that inquiry becomes more accessible for teachers and that ultimately their students see social studies as an opportunity to think and reason their way through vexing social problems and as an important staging ground for engaged citizenship.

# References

Airasian, P. W. (1991). *Classroom assessment*. New York: McGraw-Hill.

Alfieri, L., Brooks, P., Aldrich, N., and Tenenbaum, H. (2011). Does discovery-based instruction enhance learning? *Journal of Educational Psychology*, *103*(1), 1–18.

Ashby, R. (2011). Understanding historical evidence: Teaching and learning challenges. In I. Davies (Ed.), *Debates in history teaching* (pp. 137–147). New York: Routledge.

Ashby, R., Lee, P., and Shemilt, D. (2005). Putting principles into practice: Teaching and planning. In M. S. Donovan and J. D. Bransford (Eds.), *How students learn: History, mathematics, and science in the classroom* (pp. 79–178). Washington, DC: National Academies Press.

Australian Curriculum, Assessment, and Reporting Authority (no date). *Australian curriculum: History*.

Bailyn, B., and Lathem, E. (1994). *On the teaching and writing of history: Responses to a series of questions*. Hanover, NH: University Press of New Hampshire.

Bain, R. (2005). "They thought the world was flat?" Applying the principles of *how students learn* in teaching high school history. In M. S. Donovan and J. D. Bransford (Eds.), *How students learn: History, mathematics, and science in the classroom* (pp. 179–213). Washington, DC: National Academies Press.

Banchi, H., and Bell, R. (2008). The many levels of inquiry. *Science and Children*, *46*(2), 26–29.

Barrow, L. H. (2006). A brief history of inquiry: From Dewey to standards. *Journal of Science Teacher Education*, *17*(3), 265–278.

Barton, K. C. (1997). "I just kinda know": Elementary students' ideas about historical evidence. *Theory and Research in Social Education*, *25*(4), 407–430.

Barton, K. C. (2005). Teaching history: Primary sources in history—Breaking through the myths. *Phi Delta Kappan*, *86*(10), 745–748.

Barton, K. C. (2008). Research on students' ideas about history. In L. Levstik and C. Tyson (Eds.), *Handbook of research in social studies education* (pp. 239–258). New York: Routledge.

Beatty, A., Preese, C., Persky, H., and Carr, P. (1996). *U.S. history report card*. Washington, DC: U.S. Department of Education, Office of Educational Research and Improvement.

Beck, S. W., and Jeffrey, J. V. (2009). Genre and thinking in academic writing tasks. *Journal of Literacy Research*, *41*(2), 228–272. doi:10.1080/10862960902908483

Becker, C. (1958). *Modern history: The rise of a democratic, scientific, and industrialized civilization*. New York: Silver Burdett.

Bell, T., Urhahne, D., Schanze, S., and Ploetzner, R. (2010). Collaborative inquiry learning: Models, tools, and challenges. *International Journal of Science Education, 3*(1), 349–377.

Black, P., and William, D. (2009). Developing the theory of formative assessment. *Educational Assessment, Evaluation, and Accountability, 21*(1), 5–31.

Bloom, B. S. (1956). *Taxonomy of educational objectives, Handbook I: The cognitive domain*. New York: David McKay Co Inc.

Bloom, B. S. (1968). Learning for mastery. *Evaluation Comment, 1*(2), 1–12.

Bloom, B. S., Hastings, J. T., and Madaus, G. (1971). *Handbook on formative and summative evaluation of student learning*. New York: McGraw-Hill.

Boxtel, van C., and Drie, J. van (2012). "That's in the time of the Romans!" Knowledge and strategies students use to contextualize historical images and documents. *Cognition and Instruction, 30*, 113–145.

Bransford, J. D., Brown, A. L., and Cocking, R. R. (Eds.). (1999). *How people learn: Brain, mind, experience, and school*. Washington, DC: National Academy Press.

Brett, P., and Thomas, D. (2014). Discovering argument: Linking literacy, citizenship education, and persuasive advocacy. *JSSE-Journal of Social Science Education, 13*(4), 66–77.

Britt, M. A., and Aglinskas, C. (2002). Improving students' ability to identify and use source information. *Cognition and Instruction, 20*(4), 485–522.

Brophy, J., and Alleman, J. (2008). Early elementary social studies. In L. Levstik and C. Tyson (Eds.), *Handbook of research in social studies education* (pp. 33–49). New York: Routledge.

Brown, R. (1996). Learning how to learn: The Amherst project and history education in the schools. *Social Studies, 87*, 267–273.

Bruner, J. (1960). *The process of education*. New York: Vintage.

Bruner, J. (1961). The act of discovery. *Harvard Educational Review, 31*(1), 21–32.

Bruner, J. (1990). *Acts of meaning*. Cambridge, MA: Harvard University Press.

Brush, T., and Saye, J. (2002). A summary of research exploring hard and soft scaffolding for teachers and students using a multimedia supported learning environment. *The Journal of Interactive Online Learning, 1*(2), 1–12.

Brush, T., and Saye, J. (2014). An instructional model to support problem-based historical inquiry: The persistent issues in history network. *Interdisciplinary Journal of Problem-Based Learning, 8*(1), 1–13. doi:10.7771/1541-5015.1409

Campbell, D., Levinson, M., and Hess, F. (Eds.). (2012). *Making civics count: Citizenship education for a new generation*. Boston: Harvard University Press.

Caron, E. J. (2005). What leads to the fall of a great empire? Using central questions to design issues-based history units. *Social Studies, 96*(2), 51–60.

Cohen, D. (1988). Teaching practice: Plus que ca change . . . In P. Jackson (Ed.), *Contributing to educational change: Perspectives on research and practice* (pp. 27–84). Berkeley, CA: McCutchan.

Connecticut State Department of Education (2015). *Connecticut elementary and secondary social studies frameworks.* Hartford, CT: Author.

Counsell, C. (1998, May), Editorial. *Teaching History*, 3.

Counsell, C. (2000). Historical knowledge and historical skills: A distracting dichotomy. In J. Arthur and R. Phillips (Eds.), *Issues in history teaching* (pp. 54–71). London: Routledge Falmer.

Counsell, C. (2011). Disciplinary knowledge for all, the secondary history curriculum and history teachers' achievement. *Curriculum Journal*, 22(2), 201–225.

Cuban, L. (1991). History of teaching in social studies. In J. Shaver (Ed.), *Handbook of research on social studies teaching and learning* (pp. 197–209). New York: Macmillan.

Darling-Hammond, L., and Adamson, F. (Eds.). (2014). *Beyond the bubble test: How performance assessments support 21st century learning.* San Francisco: Jossey Bass.

Davis, O. L. (2001). In pursuit of historical empathy. In O. L. Davis, E. Yeager and S. Foster (Eds.), *Historical empathy and perspective taking in the social studies* (pp. 1–12). Lanham, MD: Rowman & Littlefield Publishers, Inc.

Davis, T. (2010). How I learned to stop worrying about the test and love teaching students to write well. In S. G. Grant and J. M. Gradwell (Eds.), *Teaching history with big ideas: Cases of ambitious teachers* (pp. 77–104). New York: Rowman & Littlefield.

Deboer, G. (2006). Historical perspective on inquiry teaching in schools. In L. Flick and N. Lederman (Eds.), *Scientific inquiry and the nature of science* (pp. 17–35). New York: Springer.

De La Paz, S. (2005). Effects of historical reasoning instruction and writing strategy mastery in culturally and academically diverse middle school classrooms. *Journal of Educational Psychology*, 97, 139–156.

De La Paz, S. (2013). Teaching and learning in history: Effective and reform-based practices for students with learning disabilities. *Learning Disabilities—A Contemporary Journal*, 11(1), 89–105.

De La Paz, S., and Felton, M. (2010). Reading and writing from multiple source documents in history: Effects of strategy instruction with low and average high school writers. *Journal of Educational Psychology*, 35(3), 174–192.

De La Paz, S., and Graham, S. (2002). Explicitly teaching strategies, skills, and knowledge: Writing instruction in middle school classrooms. *Journal of Educational Psychology*, 94, 687–698.

Dewey, J. (1902/1969). *The child and the curriculum.* Chicago: University of Chicago Press.

Dewey, J. (1910). Science as subject-matter and as method. *Science, 31,* 121–127.

Dewey, J. (1916/1997). *Democracy in education: An introduction to the philosophy of education.* New York: Free Press.

Dewey, J. (1938). *Experience and education.* New York: Collier.

Doolittle, P., Hicks, D., and Ewing, T. (2004). *Historical inquiry: Scaffolding wise practices in the history classroom.* Online at: www.historicalinquiry.com/inquiry/index.cfm.

Dow, P. (1970). Man: A course of study: A continuing exploration of man's humanness. In P. Dow (Ed.), *Talks to teachers* (pp. 1–16). Cambridge, MA: Education Development Center.

Dow, P. (1991). *Schoolhouse politics: Lessons from the Sputnik era.* Cambridge, MA: Harvard University Press.

Doyle, J. (2010). Big ideas and technology: A methodology to engage students. In S. G. Grant and J. M. Gradwell (Eds.), *Teaching history with big ideas: Cases of ambitious teachers* (pp. 125–140). New York: Rowman & Littlefield.

Drie, J. van, and Boxtel, C. van (2008). *Historical reasoning: Towards a framework for analyzing students' reasoning about the past,* 20(2), 87–110.

Earl, L. M. (2012). *Assessment as learning: Using classroom assessment to maximize student learning* (2nd ed.). Thousand Oaks, CA: Corwin Press.

Epstein, T. (2009). *Interpreting national history: Race, identity, and pedagogy in classrooms and communities.* New York: Routledge.

Ferretti, R., MacArthur, C., and Okolo, C. M. (2001). Teaching for historical understanding in inclusive classrooms. *Learning Disabilities Quarterly, 24,* 59–71.

Fillpot, E. (2012). Historical thinking in third grade. *Social Studies, 103*(5), 206–217.

Foels, S. (2010). Big expectations: Big ideas in honors and inclusion classes. In S. G. Grant and J. M. Gradwell (Eds.), *Teaching history with big ideas: Cases of ambitious teachers* (pp. 105–124). New York: Rowman & Littlefield.

Foster, S. J. (1999). Using historical empathy to excite students about the study of history: Can you empathize with Neville Chamberlain? *The Social Studies, 90,* 18–24.

Gerwin, D., and Visone, F. (2006). The freedom to teach: Contrasting history teaching in elective and state-tested courses. *Theory and Research in Social Education, 34*(2), 259–282.

Goodlad, J. (1984). *A place called school.* New York: McGraw-Hill.

Gradwell, J. M. (2006). Teaching in spite of, rather than because of, the test: A case of ambitious history teaching in New York State. In S. G. Grant (Ed.), *Measuring history: Cases of high-stakes testing across the U.S.* (pp. 157–176). Greenwich, CT: Information Age Publishing.

Grant, S. G. (2003). *History lessons: Teaching, learning, and testing in U.S. high school classrooms*. Mahwah, NJ: Lawrence Erlbaum Associates.

Grant, S. G. (Ed.). (2006). *Measuring history: Cases of state-level testing across the United States*. Greenwich, CT: Information Age Publishing.

Grant, S. G. (2007). Understanding what children know about history: Exploring the representation and testing dilemmas. *Social Studies Research and Practice, 2*(2), 196–208. Online at: www.socstrp.org.

Grant, S. G. (2010). High stakes testing: How are teachers responding? In W. Parker (Ed.), *Social studies today: Research and practice* (pp. 43–52). New York: Routledge.

Grant, S. G. (2013a). From inquiry arc to instructional practice: The potential of the *C3 framework*. *Social Education, 77*(6), 322–326, 331.

Grant, S. G. (2013b). From inquiry arc to instructional practice: The promise of the *College, career, and civic life (C3) framework*. In M. Herzog (Ed.), *NCSS bulletin* (pp. 25–30). Washington, DC: National Council for the Social Studies.

Grant, S. G. (2016). The problem with knowing what students know: Classroom-based and large-scale assessment in social studies. In C. Bolick and M. M. Manfra (Eds.), *Handbook of social studies research* (pp. 461–476). New York: Wiley-Blackwell.

Grant, S. G., and Gradwell, J. (2005). The sources are many: Exploring history teachers' selection of classroom texts. *Theory and Research in Social Education, 33*(2), 244–265.

Grant, S. G., and Gradwell, J. M. (Eds.). (2010). *Teaching history with big ideas: Cases of ambitious teachers*. New York: Rowman & Littlefield.

Grant, S. G., Lee, J. K., and Swan, K. (2015). *The inquiry design model*. C3Teachers. Online at: www.c3teachers.org/inquiry-design-model/.

Grant, S. G., and Salinas, C. (2008). Assessment and accountability in social studies. In L. Levstik and C. Tyson (Eds.), *Handbook of research in social studies education* (pp. 219–238). Mahwah, NJ: Lawrence Erlbaum Associates.

Grant, S. G., Swan, K., and Lee, J. (2015). Bringing the *C3 framework* to life. *Social Education, 79*(5), 310–315.

Grant, S. G., and VanSledright, B. (2014). *Elementary social studies: Constructing a powerful approach to teaching and learning* (3rd ed.). New York: Routledge.

Hammond, T. (2010). "So what?" Students' articulation of civic themes in middle-school historical account projects. *Social Studies, 101*(2), 54–59. doi:10.1080/00377990903283924

Hammond, T., and Manfra, M. (2009). Giving, prompting, making: Aligning technology and pedagogy within TPACK for social studies instruction. *Contemporary Issues in Technology and Teacher Education, 9*, 160–185.

Hartmann, U., and Hasselhorn, M. (2008). Historical perspective taking: A standardized measure for an aspect of students' historical thinking. *Learning and Individual Differences, 18*(2), 264–270.

Hartzler-Miller, C. (2001). Making sense of "best practice" in teaching history. *Theory and Research in Social Education, 29*(4), 672–695.

Hess, D. (2002). How students experience and learn from the discussion of controversial issues in secondary social studies. *Journal of Curriculum and Supervision, 17*, 283–314.

Hess, D. (2009). Controversy in the classroom: The democratic power of discussion. New York: Routledge.

Hicks, D., Doolittle, P. E., and Lee, J. (2004). History and social studies teachers' use of classroom and web-based historical primary sources. *Theory and Research in Social Education, 32*(2), 213–247.

Hicks, D., Hover, S. van, Washington, E., and Lee, J. (2011). Internet literacies for active citizenship and democratic life: In search of the intersection. In W. Russell (Ed.), *Contemporary social studies: An essential reader* (pp. 467–491). Charlotte, NC: Information Age Publishing.

Hillis, P. (2005). Assessing investigative skills in history: A case study from Scotland. *History Teacher, 38*(3), 341–360.

Hillis, P. (2008). Authentic learning and multimedia in history education. *Learning, Media and Technology, 33*(2), 87–99.

Hmelo-Silver, C., Duncan, R., and Chinn, C. (2007). Scaffolding and achievement in problem-based and inquiry learning: A response to Kirschner, Sweller, and Clark. *Educational Psychologist, 42*(2), 99–107.

Holt, T. (1990). *Thinking historically: Narrative, imagination, and understanding.* New York: College Entrance Examination Board.

Hover, S. van (2006). Teaching history in the Old Dominion: The impact of Virginia's accountability reform on seven secondary beginning history teachers. In S. G. Grant (Ed.), *Measuring history: Cases of high-stakes testing across the U.S.* (pp. 195–220). Greenwich, CT: Information Age Publishing.

Hover, S. van, and Heinecke, W. (2005). The impact of accountability reform on the "wise practice" of secondary history teachers: The Virginia experience. In E. Yeager and O. L. Davis Jr. (Eds.), *Wise social studies teaching in an age of high-stakes testing* (pp. 89–115). Greenwich, CT: Information Age Publishing.

Hover, S. van, Hicks, D., and Sayeski, K. (2012). A case study of co-teaching in an inclusive secondary high-stakes World History I classroom. *Theory and Research in Social Education, 40*(3), 260–291.

Huijgen, T., and Holthuis, P. (2015). "Why am I accused of being a heretic?" A pedagogical framework for stimulating historical contextualization. *Teaching History, 158*, 50–55.

Huijgen, T., Van Boxtel, C., Van de Grift, W., and Holthuis, P. (2014). Testing elementary and secondary school students' ability to perform historical perspective taking: The constructing of valid and reliable measure instruments. *The European Journal of Psychology of Education*, 29(4), 653–672.

Hunter, M. (1982). *Mastery teaching*. El Segundo, CA: TIP Publications.

Illinois State Board of Education. (2016). *Illinois learning standards for social science*. Springfield, IL: Author.

Jordanova, L. J. (2000). *History in practice*. London: Hodder Arnold Publication.

Kirschner, P., Sweller, J., and Clark, R. (2006). Why minimal guidance during instruction does not work: An analysis of the failure of constructivist, discovery, problem-based, experiential, and inquiry-based teaching. *Educational Psychologist*, 41(2), 75–86.

Klingner, J. K., Vaughn, S., and Schumm, J. S. (1998). Collaborative strategic reading during social studies in heterogeneous fourth-grade classrooms. *Elementary School Journal*, 99, 3–22.

Lee, J. (2010). Digital history and the emergence of digital historical literacies. In R. Diem and M. Berson (Eds.), *Technology in retrospect: Social studies' place in the information age 1984–2009* (pp. 75–90). Charlotte, NC: Information Age Publishing.

Lee, J., Doolittle, P., and Hicks, D. (2006). Social studies and history teachers' uses of non-digital and digital historical resources. *Social Studies Research and Practice*, 1(3), 291–311.

Lee, J., Manfra, M., and List, J. (2013). Things said and done: Using digital tools to enhance historical memory. In T. Lintner (Ed.), *Integrative strategies for the K–12 social studies classroom* (pp. 191–208). Charlotte, NC: Information Age Publishing.

Lee, J., and Swan, K. (2013). Is the common core good for social studies? Yes, but . . . *Social Education*, 77(6), 327–330.

Lee, J., Swan, K., and Grant, S. G. (2015). By teachers, for teachers: The NYS toolkit and C3 teachers. *Social Education*, 79(5), 325–328.

Lee, P. (2005). Putting principles into practice: Understanding history. In J. D. Bransford and M. S. Donovan (Eds.), *How students learn: History in the classroom* (pp. 31–77). Chicago: National Academies Press.

Lesh, B. (2011). *"Why won't you just tell us the answer?" Teaching historical thinking in grades 7–12*. Portland, ME: Stenhouse.

Levine, P. (2007). *The future of democracy: Developing the next generation of American citizens*. Lebanon, NH: University Press of New England.

Levinson, M. (2014). *No citizen left behind*. Boston: Harvard University Press. Medford, MA: Tufts.

Levstik, L. (1996). Negotiating the history landscape. *Theory and Research in Social Education*, 24(4), 391–415.

Levstik, L., and Barton, K. (2015). *Doing history: Investigating with children in elementary schools* (5th ed.). New York: Routledge.

Libresco, A. (2005). How she stopped worrying and learned to love the test . . . sort of. In E. Yeager and O. L. Davis Jr. (Eds.), *Wise social studies teaching in an age of high-stakes testing* (pp. 33–49). Greenwich, CT: Information Age Publishing.

Lortie, D. (1975). *Schoolteacher*. Chicago: University of Chicago Press.

Lucey, T., Shifflet, R., and Weilbacher, G. (2004). Patterns of early childhood, elementary, and middle-level social studies teaching: An interpretation of Illinois social studies teachers' practices and beliefs. *The Social Studies, 105*, 283–290.

McDiarmid, G. W. (1994). Understanding history for teaching: A study of historical understanding of prospective teachers. In M. Carretero and J. Voss (Eds.), *Cognitive and instructional processes in history and social sciences* (pp. 159–185). Hillsdale, NJ: Lawrence Erlbaum Associates.

McDiarmid, G. W., and Vinten-Johansen, P. (2000). A catwalk across the great divide: Redesigning the history teaching methods course. In P. Stearns, P. Seixas and S. Wineburg (Eds.), *Knowing, teaching, and learning history* (pp. 156–177). New York: New York University Press.

McKeown, M., and Beck, I. (1994). Making sense of accounts of history: Why young students don't and how they might. In G. Leinhardt, I. Beck and C. Stanton (Eds.), *Teaching and learning in history* (pp. 1–26). Hillsdale, NJ: Lawrence Erlbaum Associates.

McNeil, L. (2000). *Contradictions of school reform: Educational cost of standardized testing*. New York: Routledge.

Mayer, R. (2004). Should there be a three-strikes rule against discovery learning? The case for guided methods of instruction. *American Psychologist, 59*(1), 14–19.

Monte-Sano, C. (2012). What makes a good history essay? Assessing historical aspects of argumentative writing. *Social Education, 76*(6), 294–298.

Monte-Sano, C., and De La Paz, S. (2012). Using writing tasks to elicit adolescents' historical reasoning. *Journal of Literacy Research, 44*(3), 273–299.

Monte-Sano, C., De La Paz, S., and Felton, M. (2014). *Reading, thinking, and writing about history: Teaching argument writing to diverse learners in the common core classroom, grades 6–12*. New York: Teachers College Press.

Morris, R. V. (2008). A decade of plodding amongst the plots: Service learning as recognizing the contributions of others in the community. *International Journal of Social Education, 23*(2), 149–162.

National Commission on Excellence in Education. (1983). *A nation at risk*. Washington, DC: U.S. Government Printing Office.

National Council for the Social Studies (2013). *The college, career, and civic life (C3) framework for social studies state standards*. Washington, DC: National Council for the Social Studies.

National Governors Association Center for Best Practices and Council of Chief State School Officers. (2010). *Common core state standards for English language arts and literacy in history/social studies, science, and technical subjects.* Washington, DC: Author.

National Research Council (2000). *Inquiry and the national science education standards: A guide for teaching and learning.* Washington, DC: National Academy Press.

Newman, M., Degener, S., and Wu, X. (2015). *How are teachers using primary sources to meet Common Core literacy standards in English/Language arts, social studies, and science?* (NCE Research Residencies. Paper 1). Online at: http://digitalcommons.nl.edu/nce_residencies/1.

Newmann, F. M., King, B. M., and Carmichael, D. (2007). *Authentic instruction and assessment.* Des Moines, IA: Iowa Department of Education.

Newmann, F. M., Marks, H. M., and Gamoran, A. (1996). Authentic pedagogy and student performance. *American Journal of Education, 104,* 280–312.

Newmann, F. M., and Wehlage, G. G. (1993). Five standards of authentic instruction. *Educational Leadership, 50*(7), 8–12.

New York State Education Department (2014). *New York K–12 social studies framework.* Albany, NY: Author.

NGSS Lead States (2013). *Next generation science standards: For states, by states.* Washington, DC: The National Academies Press.

Nokes, J. D. (2008). The observation/inference chart: Improving students' abilities to make inferences while reading nontraditional texts. *Journal of Adolescent & Adult Literacy, 51*(7), 538–546.

Nokes, J. D., Dole, J. A., and Hacker, D. J. (2007). Teaching high school students to use heuristics while reading historical texts. *Journal of Educational Psychology, 99*(3), 492–504.

Novick, P. (1988). *That noble dream: The "objectivity question" and the American historical profession.* Cambridge, UK: Cambridge University Press.

Onosko, J., and Swenson, L. (1996). Designing issue-based unit plans. In R. Evans and D. Saxe (Eds.), *Handbook on teaching social issues* (pp. 89–98). Washington, DC: National Council for the Social Studies.

Pahl, R. (2005). July 4, 1776: The actual day of the Declaration of Independence? *The Social Studies, 96*(5), 214–215.

Pellegrino, A., and Kilday, J. (2013). Hidden in plain sight: Preservice teachers' orientations toward inquiry-based learning in history. *Journal of Social Studies Research, 4*(2), 1–26.

Piaget, J. (1962). *Play, dreams, and imitation in childhood.* New York: W. W. Norton.

Popham, W. J. (1995). *Classroom assessment: What teachers need to know.* Needham Heights, MA: Allyn and Bacon.

Ravitch, D. (2011). *The death and life of the great American school system: How testing and choice are undermining education.* New York: Basic Books.

Reisman, A., and Wineburg, S. (2008). Teaching the skill of contextualizing in history. *Social Studies, 99*(5), 202–207.

Rodriguez, H. M., Salinas, C., and Guberman, S. (2005). Creating opportunities for historical thinking with bilingual students. *Social Studies and the Young Learner, 18*(2), 9–13.

Rogers, V., and Stevenson, C. (1988). How do we know what kids are learning in school? *Educational Leadership, 45*, 68–75.

Rosenshine, B. (2012). Principles of instruction: Research-based strategies that all teachers should know. *American Educator, 36*(1), 12.

Rosenthal, R. (1987). "Pygmalion" effects: Existence, magnitude, and social effects. *Educational Researcher, 16*(7), 37–41.

Saye, J., and associates (2015). Achieving authentic pedagogy: Plan units, not lessons. In W. Parker (Ed.), *Social studies today: Research and practice* (2nd ed., pp. 65–72). New York: Routledge.

Saye, J., and Brush, T. (2005). The persistent issues in history network: Using technology to support historical inquiry and civic reasoning. *Social Education, 69*(3), 168.

Saye, J., and Brush, T. (2006). Comparing teachers' strategies for supporting student inquiry in a problem-based multimedia-enhanced history unit. *Theory and Research in Social Education, 34*(2), 183–212.

Saye, J., and Brush, T. (2007). Using technology-enhanced learning environments to support problem-based historical inquiry in secondary school classrooms. *Theory and Research in Social Education, 35*(2), 196–230.

Saye, J., and the Social Studies Inquiry Research Collaborative (SSIRC). (2013). Authentic pedagogy: Its presence in social studies classrooms and relationship to student performance on state-mandated tests. *Theory & Research in Social Education, 41*(1), 89–132.

Schug, M., Todd, R., and Beery, R. (1984). Why kids don't like social studies. *Social Education, 47*(5), 382–387.

Schwab, J. (1960). Inquiry, the science teacher, and the educator. *School Review, 68*(2), 176–195.

Schwab, J. (1978). The practical: Translation into curriculum. In I. Westbury and I. Wilkof (Eds.), *Science, curriculum, and liberal education* (pp. 365–383). Chicago: University of Chicago Press.

Shanahan, T., and Shanahan, C. (2008). Teaching disciplinary literacy to adolescents: Rethinking content area literacy. *Harvard Education Review, 78*, 40–59.

Shulman, L. (1987). Knowledge and teaching: Foundations of the new reform. *Harvard Educational Review, 57*(1), 1–22.

Smith, J., and Niemi, R. (2001). Learning history in school: The impact of course work and instructional practices on achievement. *Theory and Research in Social Education*, *29*(1), 18–42.

Stiggins, R. (1994). *Student-centered classroom assessment*. New York: Macmillan.

Stiggins, R. (2014). *Revolutionize assessment: Empower students, inspire learning*. New York: Corwin.

Stiggins, R., and Chappuis, J. (2012). *An introduction to student-involved assessment for learning* (6th ed.). Upper Saddle River, NJ: Pearson Education.

Supovitz, J. (2009). Can high-stakes testing leverage educational improvement? Prospects from the last decade of testing and accountability reform. *Journal of Educational Change*, *10*, 211–227.

Swan, K., Grant, S. G., and Lee, J. (2015). The New York state K–12 social studies toolkit: An introduction. *Social Education*, *79*(5), 309.

Swan, K., and Hofer, M. (2011). In search of technological pedagogical content knowledge (TPACK): Teachers' initial foray into podcasting in economics. *Journal of Research and Technology Education*, *44*(1), 53–73.

Swan, K., and Hofer, M. (2013). Examining student-created documentaries as a mechanism for engaging students in authentic intellectual work. *Theory and Research in Social Education*, *41*, 133–175.

Swan, K., and Hofer, M. (2014). *And action: Directing documentaries in the classroom*. New York: Rowman & Littlefield.

Swan, K., Hofer, M., and Lacascio, D. (2008). The historical scene investigation (HSI) project: Examining the use of case based historical instruction in the fifth-grade social studies classroom. *International Journal of Social Education*, *22*(2), 70–100.

Swan, K., Hofer, M., and Swan, G. (2011). Examining authentic intellectual work with a social studies digital documentary inquiry project in a mandated state-testing environment. *Journal of Digital Learning in Teacher Education*, *27*(3), 115–122.

Swan, K., Lee, J. K., and Grant, S. G. (2014). *C3 instructional shifts* (C3Teachers Briefs). Online at: www.c3teachers.org/c3shifts/.

Swan, K., Lee, J., and Grant, S. G. (2015). The New York State toolkit and the inquiry design model: Anatomy of an inquiry. *Social Education*, *79*(5), 316–322.

Swartz, R. (2008). Teaching students how to analyze and evaluate arguments in history. *The Social Studies*, *99*(5), 208–216.

Tally, B., and Goldenberg, L. B. (2005). Fostering historical thinking with digitized primary sources. *Journal of Research on Technology in Education*, *38*(1), 1–21.

Terry, A. W., and Panter, T. (2010). Students make sure the Cherokees are not removed. . .again: A study of service-learning and artful learning in teaching history. *Journal for the Education of the Gifted*, *34*(1), 156–176.

Thornton, S. (1991). Teacher as curricular-instructional gatekeeper in the social studies. In J. Shaver (Ed.), *Handbook of research on social studies teaching and learning* (pp. 237–248). New York: Macmillan.

Twyman, T., and Tindal, G. (2005). Reaching all of your students in social studies. *TEACHING Exceptional Children Plus*, *1*(5), 2–14.

Tyack, D., and Cuban, L. (1995). *Tinkering toward utopia*. Cambridge: Harvard University Press.

VanSledright, B. A. (1995). "I don't remember—The ideas are all jumbled in my head": Eighth graders' reconstructions of colonial American history. *Journal of Curriculum and Supervision*, *10*(4), 317–345.

VanSledright, B. A. (2002a). Fifth-graders investigating history in the classroom: Results from a researcher-practitioner design experiment. *Elementary School Journal*, *103*(2), 131–160.

VanSledright, B. A. (2002b). *In search of America's past*. New York: Teachers College Press.

VanSledright, B. A. (2013). *Assessing historical thinking and understanding: Innovative designs for new standards*. New York: Routledge.

VanSledright, B. A., and Brophy, J. (1992). Storytelling, imagination, and fanciful elaboration in children's historical reconstructions. *American Educational Research Journal*, *29*(4), 837–859.

VanSledright, B. A., Kelly, T., and Meuwissen, K. (2006). Oh, the trouble we have seen: Researching historical thinking and understanding. In K. Barton (Ed.), *Research methods in social studies education* (pp. 207–233). Greenwich, CT: Information Age Publishing.

VanSledright, B. A., and Limon, M. (2006). Learning and teaching in social studies: Cognitive research on history and geography. In P. Alexander and P. Winne (Eds.), *The handbook of educational psychology* (2nd ed., pp. 545–570). Mahwah, NJ: Lawrence Erlbaum Associates.

Webb, N. (1997). *Criteria for alignment of expectations and assessments on mathematics and science education* (Research monograph number 8). Washington, DC: CCSSO. Online at: http://facstaff.wceruw.org/normw/WEBBMonograph6criteria.pdf.

Wieseman, K. C., and Cadwell, D. (2005). Local history and problem-based learning. *Social Studies and the Young Learner*, *18*(1), 11–14.

Wiggins, G. (1998). *Educative assessment: Designing assessments to inform and improve student performance*. San Francisco: Jossey-Bass.

Wiggins, G., and McTighe, J. (2005). *Understanding by design* (2nd ed.). Washington, DC: Association for Supervision and Curriculum Development.

Willingham, D. (2003). Students remember . . . what they think about. *American Educator*, *27*(2), 37–41.

Willingham, D. (2007). Critical thinking: Why is it so hard to teach? *American Educator*, *31*(2), 8–19.

Willingham, D. (2009). *Why don't students like school?: A cognitive scientist answers questions about how the mind works and what it means for the classroom.* San Francisco: Jossey-Bass.

Wineburg, S. (1991). On the reading of historical texts: Notes on the breach between school and academy. *American Educational Research Journal*, *28*(3), 495–520.

Wineburg, S., and Martin, D. (2009). Tampering with history: Adapting primary sources for struggling readers. *Social Education*, *73*(5), 212–216.

Wineburg, S., and Wilson, S. (1991). Subject matter knowledge in the teaching of history. In J. Brophy (Ed.), *Advances in research on teaching* (pp. 305–347). Greenwich, CT: JAI.

Wineburg, S., Martin, D., and Monte-Sano, C. (2013). *Reading like a historian: Teaching literacy in middle and high school classrooms.* New York: Teachers College Press.

Woyshner, C. (2010). Inquiry teaching with primary source documents: An iterative approach. *Social Studies Research & Practice*, *5*(3), 36–45.

Yeager, E., and Davis, O. L. (1996). Classroom teachers' thinking about historical texts. *Theory and Research in Social Education*, *24*(2), 146–166.

Yeager, E., and Davis Jr., O. L. (Eds.). (2005). *Wise social studies teaching in an age of high-stakes testing.* Greenwich, CT: Information Age Publishing.

Yeager, E., and Foster, S. (2001). The role of empathy in the development of historical understanding. In O. L. Davis, E. Yeager and S. Foster (Eds.), *Historical empathy and perspective taking in the social studies* (pp. 13–20). Lanham, MD: Rowman & Littlefield.

# Index

Amherst Project 14, 15, 37, 41, 108
argument-making 14–16, 19–21,
    55, 60–3, 71, 83, 97–9; *see also*
    summative performance tasks
assessment 18, 55–8, 76; challenges
    56–7, 22; purposes 57–8; types
    56–7, 63–4
Authentic Intellectual Work 14–15, 108

Bailyn, Bernard 35, 36
Becker, Carl 37
Bruner, Jerome 14, 26, 42

C3Teachers.org 4, 23, 112–13
civic engagement 28, 65; *see also*
    taking informed action
Cognitive Apprenticeship Model 19
*College, Career, and Civic Life (C3)*
    *Framework for Social Studies State*
    *Standards (C3 Framework)* 3–4,
    23–4, 103–4, 107–8, 110; questions
    35, 42, 45–6, 49; sources 82, 85, 87,
    97; tasks 59, 61, 63–4, 65, 66, 69, 75
*Common Core English Language Arts*
    standards 103
compelling questions 13, 18–19,
    33–4, 36–8, 44–6, 49–50, 61–2,
    108–9; academic rigor 39–41;
    content 35–8; essential questions
    46–7; examples 36–7, 38, 40, 41,
    42, 43, 45, 47–8, 51, 55, 62, 73,
    74, 87, 85, 88, 89; 91; pedagogy
    38; student relevance 41–4, 46;
    students 49–50; tasks 55–6
*Connecticut Elementary and Secondary*
    *Social Studies Frameworks* 36

Constructive Controversies 19
content 16, 35–8, 47–8; *see also*
    disciplinary knowledge

Davis, Trisha 18
Dewey, John 13, 23, 39, 58
disciplinary knowledge 16–17, 35–8,
    59, 84, 86, 95–7
disciplinary literacy 19, 28, 103–4
disciplinary skills 16–17, 21, 59, 71,
    86, 97–8
disciplinary sources 63, 77, 81–104;
    examples 81, 83–90, 91–9, 100, 102;
    primary and secondary 20–1, 84–5;
    purposes 81–2, 111; types 86–7
discovery learning 2, 26
document-based question (DBQ) 56

formative assessment 56–7, 59; *see*
    *also* formative performance tasks
formative performance tasks 14,
    55–8, 68–74, 110–11; connection
    to compelling and supporting
    questions 55–6, 67, 68–71;
    examples 71, 72–3, 76, 91–2

Historical Scene Investigation 14,
    15, 108
historical thinking skills 21; *see also*
    disciplinary skills
Hunter, Madeline 93

IDM Blueprint 4, 24–6, 27, 58–77, 82,
    88–104, 107–9
*Illinois Learning Standards for Social*
    *Science* 36

Inquiry Arc 3, 23, 35, 107; questions 35, 46; sources 83; tasks 59, 61, 77, 81
inquiry as curriculum unit 24, 27, 33–4; examples 67, 91, 93–5
inquiry-based practice: advantages of 26–9; advocacy for 12, 18; challenges of 12, 20, 22, 25, 107; components of 107–11; elements of 13–15; expectations of teachers, students, and ideas 15–18; rationale for 12, 18–21; research on 12–13, 18–21, 107; science 13; standards 22–4; students' responses to 2–3, 12; teachers' responses to 12–13, 18–20; uncertainty 17–18; *see also* compelling questions; formative performance tasks; sources; summative performance tasks; supporting questions
Inquiry Design Model (IDM) 3, 4, 23–4, 27–29, 107–13; questions 33–5, 38, 47; sources 82, 91, 92; tasks 55–6, 58–62, 64–77

King, John 23

Lazar, Steve 112
literacy 17, 28, 104; *see also* disciplinary literacy

Man: A Course of Study 14, 108

National Assessment of Educational Progress 20
National Council for the Social Studies 3, 23
*Nation at Risk* 11
New York State K–12 Social Studies Framework 3, 35–6, 37–8

New York State K–12 Social Studies Resource Toolkit 3–4, 24, 112
Next Generation science standards 23
Niemi, Richard 20

Problem-Based Historical Inquiry 14, 15, 108
psychologizing the curriculum 39

questions 13, 18–19, 33–54, 109–10; *see also* compelling questions; supporting questions

reforms 11–12, 22

Saye, John 15
Schwab, Joseph 13, 23
Shulman, Lee 39
Smith, Julia 20
Smoot-Hawley tariff 40
Social Studies Inquiry Research Collaborative 15
sources 19–20, 81–106; adapting 101–3, 111; disciplinary nature 84–8; formative and summative tasks 85, 86, 91–2, 95, 98–9; instructional uses of 92–8, 111; literacy 103–5; primary 20–1; questions 87, 88–90; research 82–3, 85–6, 97; scaffolding 103; selecting 99–100; supporting students 99–103; *see also* disciplinary sources
staging the compelling question 74–5, 93
standards 22–4, 27–8, 36, 37–8
Stanford History Education Group 14, 108
students 2–3, 12, 16, 17, 20–1, 41–5; questions 49–50; sources 81–104; tasks 58–76

summative argument task 14,
60–5, 68–9, 71–3, 93, 110; *see also*
summative performance tasks
summative assessment 56–8, 59, 65;
*see also* summative performance
tasks
summative extensions 63–5;
examples 64, 65; *see also*
summative performance tasks
summative performance tasks 14,
57–8, 60–7, 75, 110–11; connection
to compelling and supporting
questions 55, 61; examples of 62;
formative performance tasks 71;
sources 82; *see also* summative
assessment; summative argument
task; summative extensions;
taking informed action
supporting questions 47–50, 109;
content scaffolds 47–8; examples
47–8, 70, 72, 88–90; intellectual
scaffolds 48–9

taking informed action 15, 27–28
65–7, 110; examples 66, 68
tasks 14, 19, 55–77, 75–6, 110–11;
disciplinary knowledge 59;
disciplinary skills 59; evaluation
75–7; research 56–7, 76; *see also*
formative performance tasks;
summative performance tasks
teachers 12–13, 15–16, 17–20,
21, 22; agency 28, 75, 112;
formative performance tasks
55–8, 68–74; questions 35–8, 42–5;
sources 82, 88, 92–5, 97, 99–103;
summative performance tasks
57–8, 60–7

Wineburg, Sam 14, 98